HAMPSHIRE AIRFIELDS IN THE SECOND WORLD WAR

Robin J. Brooks

COUNTRYSIDE BOOKS

NEWBURY, BERKSHIRE

First Published 1996
© Robin J. Brooks 1996

COUNTRYSIDE BOOKS
3 Catherine Road
Newbury, Berkshire

ISBN 1 85306 414 9

The cover painting shows Spitfires of no 234 (Madras Presidency)
Squadron leaving Middle Wallop airfield in the summer of 1940
from an original painting by Colin Doggett

Designed by Mon Mohan

Produced through MRM Associates Ltd., Reading
Typeset by Techniset Typesetters, Merseyside
Printed by Woolnough Bookbinding Ltd, Irthlingborough

CONTENTS

INTRODUCTION

In common with other counties in the south-east, Hampshire was to suffer badly from bomb damage during the Second World War. Although regarded mainly as a reserve area supplying troops, ships and aircraft to the more threatened counties, by the end of 1941 it was far from this with Portsmouth quickly gaining the unenviable title of the most bombed city outside London. To further protect the city and, despite the obvious dismay and objections of the islanders, an ambitious plan went ahead to illuminate Hayling Island at night to act as a decoy, and this provided Portsmouth with a certain degree of protection albeit at the expense of Hayling Island.

Many of the county's airfields performed a training role or were attached to the Fleet Air Arm. The very poor German intelligence service believed that all the airfields were fighter bases and thus placed them on their list of targets. Though most of them did receive a lot of damage, they all remained operational throughout. Without doubt however, the city of Portsmouth with its naval base and the nearby large town of Southampton with its Spitfire manufacturing facility suffered greatly.

Many of the airfields are now just memories and I have tried to recall those dramatic and hectic times. From the large military airfields to the Advanced Landing Grounds and the Flight Testing airfields, they have all played a part in forming the county's history. There are still signs to be found at most of the old airfields and of course with the army at Middle Wallop, the RAF at Odiham and the navy still very predominant in the county, one can only hope that these sites remain for future generations to discover.

It was also a war against the civilian population, for the Luftwaffe did not distinguish between military and civil targets. Bombs were dropped at random and thus the civilians of Hampshire saw the full horror and stupidity of war.

I dedicate this book to the memory of those on active service and civilians who died or were injured in the defence of the country or who were just innocent victims.

Robin J Brooks

HAMPSHIRE'S WORLD WAR II AIRFIELDS

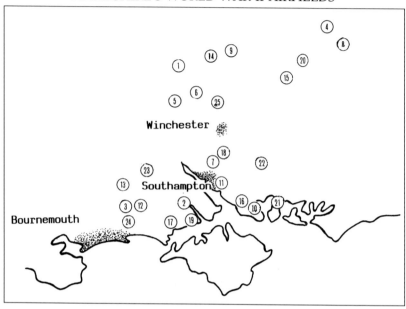

KEY TO MAP

1 Andover
2 Beaulieu
3 Bisterne
4 Blackbushe
5 Chattis Hill
6 Chilbolton
7 Eastleigh/
  Southampton
8 Farnborough
9 Frost Hill Farm
10 Gosport
11 Hamble
12 Holmsley South
13 Ibsley
14 Larks Barrow
15 Lasham
16 Lee-on-Solent
17 Lymington
18 Marwell Hall
19 Needs Ore
20 Odiham
21 Portsmouth
22 Soberton
23 Stoney Cross
24 Winkton
25 Worthy Down

I
SETTING
THE SCENE

In 1917 a total of 73 aerodromes were active in Britain. Though many of them were of a temporary nature, it indicated the vast expansion that was taking place. One year later 301 aerodromes or landing grounds were available for use but by 1924, with no more thoughts of war, the number had dropped to 44 and consisted of 27 military and 17 civilian aerodromes. Likewise the RAF had 188 operational squadrons in the immediate post-war period with 290,000 men and women within the service. Less than 14 months later, the numbers had dropped to 12 squadrons and 31,500 people. After four years of war and the belief that it would never happen again, it seemed right to discard many of the memories.

In contrast and although they had lost the war, by 1930 the Germans had embarked upon a programme of expansion. This was further accelerated on the last day of January 1933 when Adolf Hitler came to power. Not for him the ignominy of surrender but rather a forward look to the future. Although the Treaty of Versailles was intended to end German military aviation for ever, there was still a Defence Ministry that thought otherwise. By finding ways of getting around the treaty, this ministry was able to send potential German airmen to Lipezk near Moscow. It was here that a German flying school was established for the training of pilots. The whole saga was about to begin again.

In relation to the not-so-secret German build-up, Britain's air power continued to dwindle. From being the first air power in the world at the end of the war, 1933 saw it fall to fifth place. As information filtered through to Britain of the newly emerging 'Luftwaffe', a small band of prophets began to warn the nation of dire consequences ahead. The warning was heeded and on the 19th July 1934, the government announced its intention of increasing the strength of the RAF by 41 squadrons. It had suddenly become apparent that if the nation was to fight another war, it was essential to quickly expand and modernise the RAF.

A body known as the Air Ministry Works Directorate was given the main task of designing and overseeing the construction of the newly planned airfields. Their first job was to produce standard building designs for the operational as well as the domestic buildings. It is apparent even today that the neo-Georgian influence was favoured when one looks at buildings such as the officers' mess and station headquarters on many old wartime airfields still around.

The first stations to be constructed were mainly in Norfolk, Suffolk and Lincolnshire, amongst them Marham, Stradishall and Wadding-ton. Other airfields already in use were updated to current standards. In Hampshire, one of the earlier landing grounds was selected for this rapid expansion as another 100 acres was requisitioned to enlarge Odiham. Contractors Lindsey Parkinson Ltd began the work in 1934 on building new messes, H-type accommodation blocks, a new SHQ and a technical site. One item not considered then was the building of concrete runways, something which became essential as heavier aircraft arrived and the problem of waterlogging appeared. This was remedied at Odiham by 1939 and the airfield became one of the first in the country to receive concrete runways.

Now one of the largest airfields in the county, Middle Wallop was never to receive such treatment and has always remained a grass airfield. Although a 50 ft concrete perimeter track ran the entire way around the airfield, the grass landing area was considered adequate for its intended purpose. Middle Wallop was still under construction when the Battle of Britain began. Only one of the large C-type hangars had been completed and very few of the H-blocks were ready for accommodation. For the newly drafted-in airmen, it was a case of temporary conditions for some time.

On the 5th March 1936 the prototype Spitfire made its first flight from Eastleigh airport, just outside Southampton. What followed is history but powered flight had been taking place at the site since 1910 when a local man flew his 20 hp home-built aeroplane from the field. In

The designer of the Spitfire, Reginald Mitchell, surrounded by other Spitfire men at Woolston. (Crown copyright)

1918 the Americans used Eastleigh for assembling bombers to be used on operations against the German submarine bases in Belgium. The signing of the armistice on the 11th November 1918 resulted in the airfield being handed back to the RAF. With the rapid expansion in civil aviation and the interest in municipal airports towards the end of the 1920s, Southampton Corporation chose Eastleigh and work began to improve the facilities. Vickers Armstrong Ltd used the airfield for flight testing and Eastleigh was officially re-opened as Southampton Municipal Airport in November 1932. During the war it became HMS Raven of the Fleet Air Arm. When it was derequisitioned in 1946 it reverted back to a civil airport and today is the gateway to many foreign destinations.

Blackbushe was another of the airfields being built during 1940 when the Battle of Britain was at its height. Officially opened in 1942, it supported squadrons of Spitfires, Venturas, Bostons and Mosquitos, quite a mixed bag. After the war it became a major transport base and

9

was in turn used by an American Naval Facility Flight. Closed in 1960 it quickly re-emerged as a private civil aerodrome and today is popular with light aircraft flyers.

1941 also saw Lasham emerge as a satellite airfield for a bomber OTU being formed at nearby Aldermaston, but these plans were changed and the airfield became part of Army Co-operation Command. Transferred to Fighter Command in 1943 and thence to the Tactical Air Force, Lasham had a variety of aircraft and squadrons fly from its runways in support of many operations from 1942 to 1944. Like Blackbushe, it became a civil airport and gained a reputation as a very good gliding base, something that remains to this day.

One of the major aviation events in the world takes place at a Hampshire airfield. The Society of British Aircraft Constructors have held their show at Farnborough since 1948 and over the years it has risen to become one of the major shop windows for aviation. This is but a small part of its life, for experimental flying began there in 1905 with balloons. The Royal Engineers gave way to the Royal Flying Corps who operated airships until fixed wing flying began in 1914. Following the formation of the RAF the airfield was renamed the Royal Aircraft Establishment. The new title and type of work being carried out attracted the attention of the Luftwaffe and Farnborough was bombed during 1940. Despite the attention from the enemy, experimental work carried on and only after the end of the war did this commitment cease. Briefly occupied by the RAF, experimental flying and the start of the highly acclaimed SBAC shows began again in 1948 and have carried on up to the present time. Sadly the site is due for closure at any time as changing government attitudes to aviation dictate a far smaller defence force.

From 1915 there has been a strong naval presence in Hampshire. Gosport was used as a naval station between the wars. It was transferred to the Admiralty from No 16 group Coastal Command in August 1945 and though first intended to be named HMS Woodpecker, this was changed to HMS Siskin and the base used by the Service Trials Unit and the Tactical Trials Unit. Closed in 1956, the hangars and domestic buildings remain but flying is a thing of the past.

Just along the coast lies Lee-on-Solent. Another naval base in use during the first conflict, it was transferred to the Admiralty in 1939 and became HMS Daedalus. The usual collection of naval aircraft arrived. Rocs, Skuas, Swordfish, Fulmars and a Walrus for ASR work. Attacked by the Luftwaffe in August 1940, the damage was soon repaired and the base took on an experimental role as well as a training one. Under a defence review in 1981, the role of Lee was cut back but it survived total closure and is continuing in a training role today.

The last of the naval bases in the county is Worthy Down. Like Gosport and Lee, it was in use from 1917 when the RAF and the Army Co-operation School were in residence. It continued in use between the wars and was transferred to the Admiralty in 1939 becoming HMS Kestrel. Like Lee, the base was attacked in August 1940 by the Luftwaffe who thought the training base was a threat! When Eastleigh, the nearby home of the Spitfire, was attacked, development of the type was dispersed to other airfields including Worthy Down. Later much of the early trials of the Seafire, a carrier-borne version of the Spitfire, were carried out there. HMS Kestrel closed in November 1947 re-opening in June 1952 as HMS Ariel. This was a ground training establishment which closed in 1960 whereupon the navy handed the airfield over to the Royal Army Pay Corps who are still there today.

Of the remaining airfields in the county, Chilbolton still remains active. Intended as a dispersal site for the bomber base being built at Middle Wallop, it was opened in 1940 with Hurricanes of No 238 Squadron using its facilities. In use during the Battle of Britain, it was upgraded in 1942 but under-employed for its size. In 1943 the Americans flew from Chilbolton against targets in Northern France. In 1944 it was used by large transport aircraft of the USAAF to bring in wounded Americans in transit from the continent to the nearby hospital of Stockbridge. Returned to the RAF in 1945, it became an OTU with Hurricanes, Spitfires, Masters and Martinets. Now a forward airfield to Middle Wallop in No 11 Group, Spitfires and Tempests arrived to carry on the war with Japan. Luckily the armistice intervened and Chilbolton became a Flight Test Centre for Vickers Armstrong in 1947. Much of the early work on the naval Attacker was done at Chilbolton. This was followed by the Swift and in 1953, Folland Aircraft Ltd arrived to carry out trials with the Midge and later the Gnat. When they left in 1961 the airfield lay abandoned. Much of the site was later sold but part of it was retained for flying and today several fixed wing aircraft as well as helicopters use Chilbolton.

On the other hand Chattis Hill is virtually unrecognisable yet it dates back to 1917 when the RFC flew Avro 504s, BE 2cs, Pups, Spads and SE 5as. Abandoned in 1920 it was used by Supermarine in 1940 for the dispersal of Spitfires. Flying ceased in 1945 never to return and a few brick buildings in the woods surrounding the airfield are all that remain.

Though Southampton is now the main civil airport in the county, it could so easily have been rivalled by nearby Portsmouth, first visited by Alan Cobham's National Aviation Day Display on the 10th August 1932. Portsmouth Corporation had established a municipal airport on reclaimed land at Portsea Island and services began to the Isle of Wight and to Shoreham-by-Sea at the same time that Airspeed Aircraft Ltd began aircraft production from the site. Jersey Airlines became established there in 1933 and began scheduled services to the Channel Islands. The outbreak of war saw the airfield requisitioned by the Air Ministry and all civilian flying ceased. A company called Portsmouth Aviation began the overhaul and maintenance of RAF aircraft and the airfield was attacked during July 1940. No regular squadrons used the site at all during the war but aircraft from nearby Thorney Island (see *Sussex Airfields in the Second World War*) used it as well as Airspeed who had remained at Portsmouth to continue work on building the Oxford, a very popular training and communications aircraft of the period. The cessation of hostilities also brought the end of aircraft production for this aircraft but peacetime saw the return of civil flying from Portsmouth as well as Air Cadet gliding from the field. The more stringent regulations of the CAA in the post-war period regarding grass runways did nothing to encourage potential users and sadly the civilian use declined rapidly. Attempts were made in 1973 to revise its use but these failed and the airfield fell into disrepair, never to be used again.

The only remaining airfield of any significance in the county is Hamble. It is a complicated story because during its existence as a place of aviation, it has incurred many changes. Known first as a landing ground in 1913, it became the home of Fairey Aviation in 1915 and later A V Roe. Flying Boat production became very prominent at the first site as all land plane flying was transferred to Hamble Worth. Wartime saw Hamble become the home of No 3 EFTS as well as an Air Transport Auxiliary unit. No regular squadrons used the airfield but it was busy producing component parts for different aircraft throughout the war.

Its peacetime role involved giving air cadets air experience flights and a civilian flying training school was established in 1960. The last military connection at Hamble moved out in 1979 and one of the civilian schools departed to Carlisle in 1983. At the same time the receiver was called in to salvage the remains of the College of Air Training. Today the old Fairey works has become a boat-building yard and the Avro site is now a Shell storage terminal. Part of the airfield is still retained by British Aerospace who produce sub-assemblies for the Harrier and Hawk aircraft.

The last site worthy of mention is Marwell Hall which lies $3\frac{1}{2}$ miles north-east of Eastleigh town. Its position close to the Supermarine works at Eastleigh made it an ideal location for a test base for the Spitfire. Opened in 1941, in addition to Spitfire testing it also carried out modification work for various other types. During 1943 American aircraft arrived to be modified under the Lend/Lease Act and at the end of the war, the site returned to agriculture. Marwell Hall is now a zoo and is far more well known today than it was during the war. This is because Marwell Hall did not appear on any RAF map and thus remained quite secret.

This then was the airfield scene in Hampshire as war approached. The Munich crisis of 1938 proved a testing time for the airfields and squadrons and showed up many failures. Time was running short and there was still a lot to rectify. Nos 10 and 11 Groups had assumed operational and administrative control of the southern airfields including Hampshire. These groups were split into different sectors and the airfields of the county were in sector Y of No 10 Group and sector A of No 11 Group. Each sector had a sector or controlling station, in the case of Y it was Middle Wallop and in A it was Tangmere. Air Chief Marshal Sir Hugh Dowding had suggested that at least 45 fighter squadrons would be needed to ensure the safety of the UK. Out of a total number of 759 fighters only 93 were the newly acquired Hurricane, the rest were outdated biplanes. When Poland was invaded on the 1st September 1939, the RAF became fully mobilised. The air defence system was manned and the watching and waiting began.

As the war progressed, the tide slowly turned in our favour until in 1942, thoughts were in hand for an Allied invasion of the French coast. With no major new airfields being built since the late 1930s, there was a need for additional landing strips. The summer of 1942 saw a large surveying operation take place all over south-east England as the need for Advanced Landing Grounds became all too obvious. Like Kent and Sussex, Hampshire was to see a number of sites surveyed and accepted for construction. It was planned that each ALG was to have two runways of 3,000 ft roughly at right angles to each other. In order to ensure all weather serviceability, Sommerfeld Tracking, a form of metal covering laid on grass, was to be installed at each location. It was also proposed that each site should have hard-standing areas for aircraft dispersal, two Blister hangars and an area reserved for accommodation. The target date for completion was March 1943 with the work of building them being shared between the Royal Engineers Construction Groups, the RAF construction groups and the American Engineer Aviation Battalions.

Seventy-two sites were earmarked by June 1942 but this was whittled down to 36 a month later. The acquisition of the land met with fierce opposition from farmers and landowners and because of this a further nine were later abandoned. Eventually 23 were built, eight of them in Hampshire. These sites were Bisterne, Frost Hill Farm, Larks Barrow, Lymington, Needs Ore Point, Soberton, Somerton (Isle of Wight) and Winkton.

All the sites had to be ready for operations from the 1st April 1944. Farm cottages and outbuildings were requisitioned for storage space and although the majority of the men's accommodation was in tents, some of the lucky ones, usually officers, were accommodated in the cottages. As mentioned, the first metal tracking laid at the strips was Sommerfeld, named after Kurt Sommerfeld the inventor. With constant use several problems appeared, the main one being that heavy aircraft such as the American P38 Thunderbolt would rip the tracking on landing. Various other types of artificial surface were used on several ALGs; including Square Mesh Track (SMT) and the American Pierced Steel Planking (PSP).

By September 1944 as the Allies pushed forward into Europe, the ALGs had served their purpose and most of the sites had been returned to their owners and restored back to agriculture. Without such short-lived sites, D-Day would not have been the success that it was. Further sites planned as ALGs developed into full blown airfields. Concentrated in the New Forest area, they were also used for short periods, but could handle larger aircraft than the ALGs.

Today Hampshire is at peace. Odiham is still an operational RAF station and Middle Wallop is now the home of the Army Air Corps. The navy remain at Gosport and Lee-on-Solent and for the intrepid historian there are still numerous signs of a past era to be found at many of the now deserted sites. Hopefully Hampshire will see a military presence long into the future.

2
PREPARATIONS
FOR WAR

Airfield Buildings

It was known as the construction miracle. In ten short years, from 1935 to 1945, 540 permanent airfields appeared in the UK. The Hampshire airfields followed the rest of the country in receiving standard designs for the permanent buildings. The majority of them were classed as the '1935' design but it says much for the design that many of these buildings are still in use today at airfields such as Odiham and Middle Wallop. Numerous elegant examples of this period can usually be found in the officers' mess and many station headquarters. Every airfield in the county had its share of the immediate pre-war period Air Ministry timber huts. Mainly used as billets for airmen and women, these too have stood the test of time. By 1940 however, there was an acute shortage of timber and other materials were used to provide accommodation. Two of the more familiar huts still around today are the Maycrete which was built of concrete and the Nissen, a combination of wood and corrugated sheeting. The latter design actually originated from the First World War and was designed by Colonel P Nissen. Revived for the second conflict, many of them survive in situ today on the county's airfields. Later on when materials

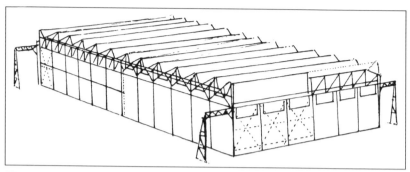

Hangar type 'C'. (C. Sampson)

became even scarcer, a company manufactured the very handy Handcraft Hut which was roofed with asbestos cement sheeting. There are many other types which came as the airfields developed but from 1944 onwards, with the prospect of peace around the corner, these types eventually gave way to bricks. Many of the Maycretes and Nissens still survive and are used for a variety of purposes.

Hangar designs are varied on the airfields. Before the rapid pre-war expansion period, the 'A' type was the most prominent. Built with doors at each end, it had a length of 250 ft with a height of 25 ft. As aircraft grew in size larger hangars became necessary and by 1935 a new type known only as the 'C' type came into production. Several fine examples of the 'C' are still to be seen at Middle Wallop. With a length of 300 ft and a span of 150 ft, most of the expansion airfields received between two and six of them.

Being very large hangars, their construction took up a lot of precious time. With this in mind two hangars of similar size but much simpler construction were designed and built by the steel firm Sir William Arrol and Co Ltd. Named the 'J' and 'K' types, they were metal with a curved roof of steel plate. An added advantage was that rooms were attached alongside the hangar to be used as offices, stores or even crew rooms.

To meet the ever-changing conditions and needs of the expansion airfields, 400 Bellman Transportable hangars were produced between 1938 and 1940. With a 95 ft span and 180 ft long, they provided a very necessary stop-gap in aircraft protection between some of the other designs.

Yet another type was produced in 1940 when the Air Ministry

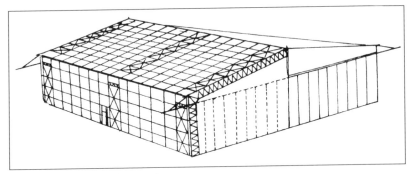

Hangar type 'T2'. (C. Sampson)

together with the Tees-side Bridge and Engineering Works designed and built a hangar that is still to be seen at many airfields today. Known as the 'T' type, the 'T' standing for transportable, it was easily constructed, easy to take down and to re-assemble. Unlike the 'J' and 'K' types it had no buildings alongside but its cheapness to produce and the simplicity of the design more than made up for this. The design

The Blister hangar was to be seen at many of the airfields, this one is a particularly good example.

17

proved so useful that 906 'T' types were constructed on RAF stations both in the UK and abroad.

Without doubt however, it was the Blister hangar that gave each airfield its character. Produced by Messrs C Miskins and Sons in 1939, it was given a trial at Biggin Hill airfield in Kent. Proving very successful and again being cheap and easy to produce, over 3,000 were soon supplied to the RAF.

Though the hangars were an integral part of the wartime airfield, it must surely be the control tower that evokes most nostalgic feelings. Prior to 1939, air traffic control in the RAF was very minimal. It was the duty of pilots to log with the duty station officer their intentions. All of this changed with the expansion, and provisions were made for a special type of office to be built for this purpose. Known as the watch office, it was initially a single-storey building but larger airfields had two or even three levels. During 1941 it was felt that a standard design was needed to cover all operational airfields and the watch office gradually gave way to the control tower. Known as Type 12779/41, it has probably become the most well known of all wartime towers. Middle Wallop has a fine example of a late wartime pattern control tower which was adapted post-war with the addition of a glass visual control room added to the second level. This gives an all-round visual control of the airfield for the modern day operational base.

Defence and Camouflage

During the first conflict it was not considered necessary to defend the airfields or to apply camouflage to buildings and landscape. This changed in 1937 and experiments in airfield camouflage were carried out at Cranwell under the direction of Colonel Sir John Turner. He decided that in order to confuse the enemy from the air it was necessary to paint buildings a similar colour to the surrounding area. Hence grass landing areas became just a collection of fields and hedges by painting heavy black lines on the grass whilst the dispersal of aircraft amongst the trees and woods around the perimeter made sure that no eagle-eyed enemy noticed them alongside the lines!

Mainly brown, green and black paint was used for the subterfuge and practically everything white was painted. Thus neat kerbstones painstakingly painted white by junior airmen during the inter-war period were hastily blacked out. As if to emphasise the point, an incident at an airfield on the Hampshire/Sussex border added fuel to the contention that camouflage was badly needed.

For some considerable time in 1940 the Luftwaffe bombers had crossed the coast between the two borders. When the night attacks began, it seemed that every time there was a bright moon the majority of enemy aircraft flew directly over the airfields of the two counties. No one quite knew why until a British night-fighter pilot happened to mention one day that the concrete runways of Tangmere and Odiham had helped him to find his own base. The penny dropped! The enemy aircraft had also seen the white runways as though it were daylight. Immediately gangs of civilian workmen were engaged to paint the runways green so that they blended with the surrounding countryside.

Duly employed, the British workmen did not exactly put themselves out and progress was painfully slow. Another period of moonlight was approaching and it was feared by the authorities that eventually the airfields would be a target themselves. As the workmen could not be spurred into working faster and finishing the job that much quicker, a certain fighter pilot felt that drastic action was required.

The pilot was Douglas Bader and it was he who asked a journalist friend to write an article on the lack of co-operation between civilians and the military. The next weekend an article appeared in a newspaper about two RAF airfields being endangered by British workmen not putting their backs into the job. The Air Ministry were not amused and demanded to know from whom the writer had got his facts. The information was not of course forthcoming but a short time later when the Under-Secretary of State for Air paid a visit to Tangmere, he mentioned to Group Captain Woodhall, the station commander, and Douglas Bader that as the Air Ministry did not take a good view of it, he had actually come down to give someone a rocket over the article. Douglas immediately jumped on the defensive and told him to take the rocket back to the Ministry and tell them what they could do with it! He continued by saying that the runways had been shining for months now enticing the German bombers to attack. Somewhat taken aback, the Under-Secretary promised to look into the matter and within weeks, with the promise of a bonus at the end, the workmen had camouflaged the runways of Tangmere and Odiham.

Undoubtedly camouflage was to prove most effective during the war. The ultimate deception was to construct dummy or decoy airfield sites close to the operational base itself. These came roughly into two categories with a 'K' site having dummy aircraft and buildings and a 'Q' site being equipped with fake Drem runway lighting. The Drem system replaced the old 'goose-neck' paraffin lamps and was developed by the Mechanical and Electrical Engineering Division of the Air Ministry. On a real airfield it comprised three parts — the actual runway lighting itself, the approach lighting and the over circle lighting — all controlled by a single switch.

The first decoys were operational in January 1940 and by August of that year, 26 'K' and 56 'Q' sites were in use with 406 dummy aircraft built to populate them. In September, decoy machine gun posts were even added to the 'K' sites. The idea eventually spread to lighting decoy fires on the outskirts of towns and cities to confuse the enemy bombers. Named 'Starfish', an in-depth description of this deception is outside the bounds of this book but it is worthy of mention to give an overall picture.

The decoy programme cost millions of pounds but the success of the idea made the expense worthwhile. This may be judged by the fact that by 31st July 1940, 60 enemy attacks had been made on 30 sites whilst only ten were made on parent airfields. In Hampshire the four main airfields to receive decoy sites were as follows:-

Middle Wallop — Decoy airfield at Houghton.

Andover — Decoy airfield at Hurstbourne.

Odiham — Decoy airfield at Froyle.

Worthy Down — Decoy airfield at Micheldever.

Also worthy of mention is the Hayling Island decoy, set up to confuse the enemy attacks around Portsmouth airfield with its aircraft factory. When the residents of Hayling Island realised that their homes were a decoy for Portsmouth, they mounted a vociferous campaign to stop the idea from blossoming. Unfortunately the authorities insisted and the plan went ahead. The decoy fires and lights were placed as far as possible from the more populated area and there was no recorded loss of life. On the night of 17/18th April 1941, when a heavy force of bombers attacked the Hampshire area, the decoy took 90% of the bombs intended for Portsmouth. In all, 26 mines, 170 HE bombs, 20 oil bombs and thousands of incendiaries were dropped on Hayling Island. By 1942, as the attacks on airfields and aircraft factory sites became less frequent and the decoy sites became known to the enemy, the sites gradually became obsolete. Very little remains today to remind us of a very important part of the overall deception plans.

The 1939/45 standard 90 cm search-light. (C Samson)

Preparations for the defence of the airfields took a long time in coming. Even by 1939 the protection of operational sites was confined to one or two machine-gun posts. Not until the evacuation at Dunkirk was it realised that the enemy's might would soon be turned upon the airfields of Britain. Once again the Air Ministry's Directorate of Works was given the task of building up these defences.

Many airfields made up their own defences in the early days using antiquated machine-guns mounted on the backs of trucks or lorries. These were usually constructed by the airmen themselves but the main defence of the airfields was generally left to the Royal Artillery with Bofors guns. Pillboxes were hastily built around the perimeter and were manned day and night. In 1940 the General Staff Headquarters of Army Southern Command issued a set of instructions which forewarned both the RAF and the army gunners of what they could expect in the event of an attack. Paragraph 9 stated: 'Should any high bombing take place, do not let the whistling bomb scare you. It is no

The semi-sunk pillbox. (C Samson)

more dangerous than any other bomb'. Small comfort in the early days of war.

Later on some stations were issued with armoured cars called Armadillos which were equipped with a 1.5 pounder gun and machine guns. These were supplemented by a smaller vehicle called a Beaverette which supported just one machine-gun. To operate the guns used for airfield defence, the Air Ministry created a new trade, that of gunner. Most of the recruits were trained at No 1 Ground Defence Gunnery School at Ronaldsway on the Isle of Man and were the forebears of the RAF Regiment which was formed in 1943.

If necessity is the mother of invention, then war must surely bring out the best in inventors. Several very far-fetched ideas were forthcoming in the defence of the airfields. The Pickett-Hamilton Retractable Fort was one. Designed to provide an element of surprise to landing enemy paratroopers, it consisted of a round concrete cylinder with firing slits mounted inside a larger concrete cylinder. This inner cylinder supported two airmen equipped with guns who could lower or raise this section of the fort by means of either pumping a handle or by releasing compressed air into the raising mechanism from a cylinder. Entry to the fort was by a hatch in the top which when shut, and with the fort in the lowered position, gave no indication to the enemy that it was there. Churchill himself saw a demonstration of this retractable fort and put his full support behind it. Such was his influence that by 1941, 170 had been installed at 59 airfields including Middle Wallop and Odiham. They were however never used in anger and by the end of 1941 were considered useless due to flooding and problems with getting the fort to raise. Many remain in situ today and are a constant source of discovery for historians.

Another strange invention was the Parachute and Cable Device

The Pickett-Hamilton Retractable Fort was in situ at many airfields including Middle Wallop. Here the author is about to descend into a fort.

(PAC) which was mainly installed at fighter airfields. It consisted of a steel cable which was fired into the air by rockets whereupon a parachute was released and the cable slowly descended back to earth. The hope was that any enemy aircraft attacking an airfield would fly into one of these cables and crash to earth. It is not recorded just how effective this wild idea was!

Even in 1942, the threat of enemy paratroopers landing was still prevalent. In the event that it did happen, it was obviously necessary to deny them any use of the airfields. One way to do this would be to blow up the grass landing areas and the concrete runways of the more modern airfields. The two main methods of airfield denial were known as the Canadian Pipe Mine system and the Mole Plough. It was the former that came to be used on airfields with hard runways and consisted of a series of steel pipes buried in the concrete. These were packed with explosive and could be detonated from a single point if the need arose.

Likewise the Mole Plough system was a series of explosive-packed rubber strips that could be laid in furrows on a grass airfield and

23

covered over. More than 20 airfields were equipped with pipe mines of either type, some of them still being taken out today. One of the most recent removals took place at Detling airfield in Kent when the Royal Engineers sealed off the entire area in case they detonated. Early experiments in the pipe mine system were carried out at Odiham, Blackbushe and Farnborough but once again, the idea was never used in anger. Today, airfield defence is in the capable hands of the RAF Regiment with their Rapier ground to air missiles, all of this a far cry from the ad-hoc weapons and inventions of 1940.

Radar and the Royal Observer Corps

When the Battle of Britain began there were 21 operational Chain Home radar stations and 30 Chain Home Low stations. Sited on coastline cliffs or on high ground some distance inland, the giant lattice towers played an integral part in defeating the Luftwaffe during those early dark days.

The early warning system was conceived as far back as the 1920s when a series of concrete sound mirrors were erected along the south coast. These huge concave slabs reflected the sound of aero engines approaching from the sea but usually only under perfect weather conditions. Unfortunately they also picked up the noise of car engines passing nearby thus confusing the listening operator. For many years the problem seemed insoluble until a government committee, the Scientific Survey of Air Defence, invited Robert Watson-Watt of the National Physical Laboratory at Teddington to outline his proposals and findings in radio location. So impressed were the committee with his presentation that money was immediately made available for an experimental station to be set up at Orford Ness on the Suffolk coast.

As history tells us, these experiments were a success and by the summer of 1936 when Air Chief Marshal Sir Hugh Dowding took up his new post at the head of the air defence organisation, the first metal towers were being erected around the south-east coastline. The headquarters for the new defence system was established in an old mansion at Stanmore in north-west London. Known as Bentley Priory, it was to become the hub of an operation that would eventually win the Battle of Britain and lead Britain to victory.

Initially the system was called Radio Location or Radio Direction Finding, the term Radar coming later when the Americans entered the war. By 1936, five sites were given the go-ahead to cover the Thames estuary. The training of personnel to operate the RDF stations began a year later at Bawdsey and in the same year the newly opened sites took part in air exercises. Despite a few problems the system worked well and treasury approval was given to expand the RDF stations to 20. These were to be known as Chain Home stations but originally were more commonly called AMES 1 (Air Ministry Experimental Station 1). Included in this first 20 was Ventnor on the Isle of Wight but negotiations with local landowners held up the commencement of work. It was the Munich crisis that generated new life into the programme as the date for the beginning of the system was set at 1st April 1939. In view of the deteriorating situation, it was decided to compulsory purchase the land needed and to attempt to persuade the tower construction companies to work 24 hours a day, seven days a week. Work on Ventnor began immediately and along with the other 19 stations, it was to receive a 360 ft steel tower which supported the aerial array whilst a 240 ft wooden tower would carry the receiver array. Electrical power was to be taken from the National Grid with each station having a stand-by generator in case bombing brought the power lines down or severed the underground cables. When war was declared on 3rd September 1939, all 20 CH stations were on the air.

After the compulsory purchase order went ahead for Ventnor, the construction gangs moved in and began to dig out the foundations for the control rooms, generator room, accommodation block, air raid shelters and all the other buildings needed to survive an attack. Tarmac roads had to be laid between buildings for it must be remembered that much of this land was farmland. With the exception of duty personnel, the operating and engineering staff were housed some distance from the station in an attempt to reduce the number of casualties expected to occur during an air raid. The site was originally protected by soldiers who lived in huts around the perimeter but this duty was gradually taken over by the RAF Regiment. As there was very little fire-power with which to protect the site, a raid on Ventnor on the 12th August 1940 destroyed the majority of the buildings and put the station out of action for some days. The unexploded bombs caused the entire staff to evacuate the site, thus causing a large gap in the radar protection screen. Just as it got back on the air, another devastating attack took place which wrecked many of the underground buildings and again

Though the photo is of Dunkirk radar station in Kent, Ventnor on the Isle of Wight had the same structures with the control rooms situated beneath the aerial array. (S E Newspapers)

put the station out of action. This time a mobile reserve station was set up at Bembridge on the island to cover the gap. Luckily the Luftwaffe were not aware that they had caused Ventor to go off the air.

During exercises in 1939, it had been found that the radar cover did not extend to low level and an aircraft flying low could easily avoid detection. Extra RDF stations were therefore built to cover this problem, these becoming known as Chain Home Low (CHL) stations. None were built in Hampshire but coverage from a CHL station at Worth Matravers in Dorset on one side and Beachy Head in Sussex on the other ensured that the county had low level protection.

Most of the CH and CHL radar stations were dismantled during the 1950s as newer types of radar coverage came along but many concrete blocks and shelters associated with them remain to this day.

Together with the RDF systems it was the Observer Corps which contributed to Britain's early warning system. This vital arm of our defence strategy came very cheaply, for the Corps consisted mainly of volunteers eager to do their bit for the country. When it came under the wing of the Air Ministry in 1929, there began a close relationship with the RAF which was sadly severed with the stand-down of the Corps in 1991. It was in itself a primitive type of operation which but for the insistence of Dowding that it was necessary to the defence of the country may well have floundered in its infancy. When Winston Churchill described the techniques of the Observer Corps as 'stone age', it was the chief of Fighter Command who sprang to its defence.

Conceived by General E B Ashmore in 1917, the system of reporting the tracks of aircraft was in full working order by the late summer of 1918. The armistice did not stop the work and the idea of a chain of reporting posts with the title 'Air Defence Observation in the Weald of Kent — 1924' continued. The experiments in Kent proved successful and General Ashmore was keen to expand the observing to a larger area. Accordingly he planned exercises to cover Kent, Sussex and Hampshire with operations rooms in all three counties. The majority of posts were placed close to a telephone exchange and with the enrolment of special constables completed, exercises were planned for the 22nd and 24th June 1925.

With three RAF squadrons participating, the observers managed to track many of the aircraft successfully. Such was the success that the ARP committee recommended even further extentions to the system to cover all the home counties. The air exercises of the 25th July 1927 gave a chance for the network to be tried under very realistic conditions. The

27

RAF provided two groups, one to represent the attackers and the other to be the defence forces. Tangmere supplied Nos 1 and 43 Squadrons equipped with Siskins and Gamecocks respectively and together with several other units from different airfields, formed the interceptor force. Again it proved a great success and the Corps Commander-in-Chief sent a congratulatory telegram to the chief constables referring to the corps as 'being invaluable to the Commander of the defending forces'.

All of this helped General Ashmore in his decision that more observer personnel would be needed and he raised the post strengths to at least eight members in order to establish a 24 hour rota basis.

As the great build-up for war gathered pace, in 1937 the Observer Corps were still the only accurate means of early warning as radar was not yet operating on a national basis. The biggest test of the system so far was in 1938 when the annual home defence exercises were held from the 5th to the 7th August. That same year the Munich crisis put them on full alert and at 4 pm on Monday 26th September, the corps were called out and put on a wartime footing. This situation continued until the 1st October 1938 when Neville Chamberlain returned from Germany with his infamous piece of paper. That same day the corps was stood down.

Many problems had been highlighted during the war footing period, one of them being that with a 24 hour seven days a week operation, some sort of living accommodation was needed for the observers. It was decided that wooden huts with cooking and sleeping facilities were the answer and accordingly, construction of them began all over the country.

By early 1939 everything was in place and by the time war was declared, the corps had already been on full time duty for eight days and nights. The 'Phoney War' gave another welcome period of adjustment so that by the time the real war began in 1940, the observers had become even more proficient. The Battle of Britain proved their worth and in 1941, the corps rightfully received its 'Royal' prefix.

Hampshire came within No 3 Group of the ROC with its command headquarters at Winchester. Formed in 1926, it remained within 3 Group until 1953 when it was re-designated No 14 Group. The location of the headquarters changed over the years. From 1926 until 1929 it was at the Blue Triangle Club in Parchment Street, from 1929 to 1940 in the Brook Street telephone exchange, from 1940 to 1943 in Northgate House in Jewry Street and from 1943 to stand-down in 1991, in Abbots

Road, Winchester. A total of 48 outside posts were built initially although this reduced as peacetime requirements became less. The uneasy peace that followed the war also led the ROC onto a new field, that of reporting nuclear fall-out in the event of atomic and hydrogen warfare. In 1960, the post and command centres went underground as a protection for themselves against nuclear fall-out. This role continued until 1991 when under a government review, the corps was stood down though not disbanded.

The spirit lives on and there is no doubt that although not active the observers of today are as proud of their achievements as were their predecessors in 1939.

This then was the scene as Hampshire prepared to go to war. Within its borders were military targets that would certainly receive the attention of the Luftwaffe; the great naval base at Portsmouth, the aircraft manufacturing plants at Eastleigh and of course the fighter airfields. Alongside the neighbouring counties of Sussex and Dorset, Hampshire would be in the forefront of the battle. Its military personnel and its civilian population would come to know the full horrors of war first hand. This is part of that story.

3
ANDOVER

During its existence as an airfield, Andover had the dubious honour of being firstly a bomber station, secondly a fighter station and thirdly an army co-operation airfield. It remains as the latter today, with fixed wing and rotary aircraft of the Army Air Corps from Middle Wallop frequently seen on its lush grass.

Andover opened in August 1917 as a bomber station. Several canvas Bessoneaux hangars and tented crew rooms were erected as Nos 104, 105 and 106 Squadrons flew in with a very mixed bag of aircraft including DH9s, BE 2bs and RE 8s. No 148 joined them briefly on the 10th February 1918 before the squadrons departed to France and Ireland respectively whereupon Andover took on a training role for a brief period.

1920 saw the RAF Staff College established there together with No 7 Group to administer army co-operation squadrons in Hampshire. Several squadrons were rotated through the base over the next few years as Andover became the Air Navigation School in January 1935. A day bomber unit in the form of No 142 Squadron flying Hawker Harts arrived from Netheravon but embarked for the Middle East in October 1935 during the Abyssinian crisis. The squadron returned to Andover on 3rd December 1936 and was joined by No 12 Squadron with the Hawker Hind. These two units were to remain associated with the base for many years.

The Fairey Battle, a light day bomber, was announced as the answer to every pilot's prayers when it came to a modern aircraft. It presented a great advance over the Hawker biplanes and was warmly received by the air force. It did not however live up to expectations and although

Another potent enemy, the Dornier DO217E. (MAP)

the prototype Battle first flew in March 1936 with the first production aircraft flying a year later, by 1939 the type was obsolete. Underpowered by its single Rolls Royce Merlin 1 engine and under-armed with its one Browning gun forward and one Vickers gun aft, it did have its moments of glory when a Battle gunner claimed the first German aircraft shot down during the war and the RAF's first two VCs were won by Fairey Battle pilots. Unfortunately it was soon transferred to training and target towing duties but when first received by No 12 Squadron at Andover, the pilots thought it the 'bee's knees'.

In March 1938, No 142 converted to the Battle and together with No 12 formed No 76 Bomber Wing. Andover prepared itself for war by camouflaging all obvious buildings, digging shelters and building gun sites. Whilst other squadrons had taken their Battles to war in France, 76 remained at Andover until the station was transferred from Bomber to Fighter Command in May 1940. With the evacuation of troops from Dunkirk and the Germans now in possession of the French Channel ports, it was felt that more fighter airfields were needed back here.

Andover became part of No 22 Group, Army Co-operation Command. Under the new group, the Battles left for Bicester to be replaced by the Hectors and Blenheims of No 59 Squadron. This unit had been forced out of France by the rapid German advance but it continued to operate over the Continent carrying out bombing raids on the Channel ports together with anti-submarine missions.

With the start of another global war, the Staff College closed and did not reform until sometime later. Although enemy aircraft passed overhead frequently, it was not until 13th August that the airfield was on the target list. Although Eagle Day got off to a bad start for the Luftwaffe, the afternoon raids were a different story. LG1 operating from Orleans/Bricy sent 80 JU 88s towards Portland. As the formation approached the Hampshire coast it split, some attacking Southampton whilst five spotted Andover airfield in the distance. Coming in low, the 88s dropped bombs on the SHQ, the parade ground and the landing area; three men were killed and six Blenheims were damaged. The Hurricanes of No 238 Squadron from Middle Wallop bore into the attack, the trails of hectic dogfighting beginning to form across the Hampshire sky. Within minutes, three of the squadron were fighting for their lives as the German fighters did their best to protect the bombers. Sgt E W Seabourne in Hurricane P3764 attempted to leave his blazing aircraft but hit the sea before he could get out. Although burnt, he was rescued from the water and lived to fight another day. Another Sgt pilot, Tony Marsh, went missing when he was shot down somewhere over the county, and is one of many remembered on the Runnymede Memorial.

Work went on at Andover all night to clear the debris. Although it was not a major fighter airfield, a decoy was laid out at Hurstbourne, some seven miles away. This was built too late to stop a further raid on Andover on the 14th August when a single enemy aircraft flew overhead and dropped anti-personnel bombs. Although only one aircraft was involved, it cost two lives on the ground.

No 59 Squadron had moved to Odiham on the 9th June 1940. No 81 had come and gone with their Avro Rotas, a Cierva autogiro used for army co-operation work. From this time on no resident operational squadrons were at Andover but No 2 School of Army Co-operation were still flying Ansons and Blenheims for training in low flying and photography.

1941 saw very little change but the airfield was attacked on two occasions resulting in severe damage to the hangars which later had to be demolished entirely. The School of Army Co-operation was split, part of it going to Thornaby whilst the section left at Andover formed the nucleus of No 42 Operational Training Unit, which was given the task of converting Lysander crews to the Blenheim. This continued for the rest of 1941 and it was not until 25th October 1942 that a resident

A P38 Lockheed Lightning, the type used at Andover during the latter part of the war. (MAP)

squadron arrived at Andover. No 296 flew their Whitley Vs over from Hurn. Built by Armstrong Whitworth, the Whitley, together with the Hampden and Wellington, was the mainstay of Bomber Command in the early years of the war. The type was finally retired from front line service in 1942 but served in a variety of other roles until late 1943 and beyond. One of these duties was leaflet dropping, a task that 296 carried out from Andover. Never was a squadron motto of 'Prepared for all things' more apt!

The bombers were joined by a tactical reconnaissance unit in the same month when No 170 Squadron flew their Mustang fighters in from Thruxton. The new year saw No 16 bring their Mustangs to Andover heralding a period of intense activity. Even the FAA came to train with the army squadrons but by December 1943, Andover was left with just one unit as the Mustangs moved to fighter airfields to do combat with the increasing number of enemy fighter/bombers that were attacking the coastal towns.

Andover's single runway was now 3,900 ft long and still grass but with very good drainage in winter. It could accommodate most aircraft. In February 1944 it was really put to the test when one of the heaviest fighter aircraft at that time arrived at the base. In March 1940, the RAF ordered a total of 143 Lockheed Lightning Is. This heavy, twin boom fighter powered by two 1,475 hp Allison V-1710-11Y in-line engines was a new concept and design for a fighter. Its design and performance so impressed the Ministry that 143 were ordered with the first production aircraft being delivered in December 1941. Tested at Boscombe Down, the aircraft was rejected by the RAF and handed back to the USAAF. A further order for 524 Lightning Mk II fighters was cancelled and although the type never flew in RAF markings, several USAAF units flew them from Britain.

The 370th Fighter Group was one of the three Lightning equipped fighter units of the 9th Air Force. After arriving in this country during February 1944, the group and its three squadrons, the 401st, 402nd and 485th became operational at Andover on 1st May 1944. They immediately began dive bombing attacks on enemy radar stations and marshalling yards in preparation for the D-Day landings. Although a large aircraft, only two mishaps occurred of any consequence, both of them due to overshooting the relatively short runway. The Lightnings however did tear up the grass on several occasions.

On the 6th June 1944, the group's aircraft provided top cover over the invading allies. This continued for a week and the unit finally moved to the Continent on 20th July, the airfield returning to the fold of the RAF nine days later.

The Americans however were the last operational squadrons to use the airfield. For Andover, the war was nearly over as a training unit with Austers moved in. This was the first of the many Air Observation Post squadrons which were to use the base until 1945. When peace finally came, the RAF Staff College returned accompanied by a communications squadron. The next 15 years continued in a similar vein until 1960 when No 225 Squadron formed at Andover with Sycamore and Whirlwind helicopters. In later years, Pembroke and Basset aircraft used the field but finally, in the 1975 Defence Review, No 21, the last squadron to use Andover, was axed and with it the airfield. In 1977 the army took over the site and today, as already noted, they are still in occupation. Although flying is very restricted, at least Andover has not gone the usual path of commercial development.

4

BLACKBUSHE

With approach radar and instrument landing systems in use at the majority of military and civil airfields, today's pilots have no fear of fog. In 1944 however, no such aids existed and fog dispersal to allow aircraft to land safely when pilots had difficulty in seeing the ground was left to an invention known as FIDO, Fog Investigation and Dispersal Operations. The equipment consisted of petrol burners installed at short intervals along the runway. When these burners were lit, the heated air rose and dispersed the fog sufficiently for aircraft to land. Several airfields received the system during 1944 but for Blackbushe, it was to be May 1948 before FIDO was installed.

The type used was a Haigill Mk 5 surface type system, not the more widely used sub-surface installation. In the event it was only used once in anger when a Vickers Viking of Airwork took off under bad conditions. The system was withdrawn about 1959 and eventually Blackbushe was equipped with a modern landing system.

Also known as Hartfordbridge Flats, the airfield began life in October 1941 when a site was requisitioned, situated five miles west of Camberley alongside the main A30 road. The building firm of McAlpines were engaged to construct a three-runway bomber airfield. Previously the site had been used by the nearby Royal Aircraft Establishment at Farnborough for glider trials, this continuing whilst the airfield was being built. Hartfordbridge was officially opened on the 1st November 1942 and was attached to No 70 Group. It is interesting to note that it had taken McAlpines just over a year to construct a very large airfield. This was a far cry from the early expansion period of 1938/39 when the civilian workmen and the

FIDO in action. Blackbushe was one of the airfields that had the system installed. (F/O Frazer)

military construction gangs were constantly at each others throats. The RAE became the first occupants but on the 7th December 1942 No 171 (AC) Squadron brought their Tomahawk Is and Mustang IAs over from Gatwick. They began flying reconnaissance missions along the French coast but were disbanded on the 1st February 1943 to form the nucleus of No 430 Squadron. It was re-equipped with the Tomahawk and departed to Dunsfold on the 8th January 1943 leaving the contractors to complete much of the unfinished work at Hartford-bridge.

By the spring the airfield was complete and on the 16th March 1943 No 140 Squadron moved their Blenheims from Mount Farm for a long stay. Gradually the faithful Blenheims were replaced by the Lockheed Venturas and conversion to the type began immediately. A development of the Lockheed Lodestar transport aircraft, the Ventura was gradually to replace the Blenheim and the Hudson in many roles. Although a British contract for 675 Ventura Mk I and Mk II bombers was placed in the summer of 1940, deliveries ceased with the 394th aircraft. 140 Squadron was among one of the first to receive the type but very few operations were carried out in them before they eventually gave way to the far superior De Havilland Mosquito. Two marks were allocated to 140, the earlier Mk IX and the later XVI. With a

Messerschmitt ME109Es line-up at a French airfield. (MAP)

maximum speed of 380 mph at 17,000 ft, they were used in the photographic reconnaissance role with the squadron.

On the 29th June 1943, 140 were joined by No 16 Squadron equipped with PR Spitfires and together they formed No 34 (PR) Wing. This was in preparation for the planned allied invasion of Europe and both squadrons carried out photographic missions from a high level as well as low level.

Intense security was evident at the airfield during August 1943 as the Venturas of No 21 Squadron and the Bostons of Nos 88 and 107 Squadrons flew in to form a No 2 Group Wing. They immediately began flying missions connected with Operation 'Starkey', the large scale deceptive operation carried out over the Pas de Calais in September 1943. The idea was that the intense activity over this region would fool the enemy into thinking that any invasion plans would include a landing in the Pas de Calais region. The squadrons carried out bombing raids on airfields, train yards and ammunition dumps in an attempt to confuse the enemy. Sadly 107 Squadron lost two Bostons shot down by ground defences but there is no doubt that 'Starkey' helped to convince the German High Command that this region was earmarked for an allied assault. This was a very hectic period for the airfield with various arrivals and departures, No 21 Squadron was there briefly from 19th August to 27th September, No 88 also arrived on 19th August but stayed until 16th October 1944, and 107 Squadron's sojourn was from 20th August to February 1944.

When 21 Squadron left Hartfordbridge on the 27th September 1943 for Sculthorpe, their place was taken by No 342 (Free French) Squadron named 'GB 1/20 Lorraine'. They brought their Boston IIIAs down from Great Massingham on the 6th September 1943 and converted to the Boston IV shortly after. This mark had the addition of a power operated dorsal turret giving the aircraft extra fire-power. Flying daylight raids on targets in northern France in all weathers, the squadron motto of 'Here we are' became very apt! Daylight operations did however hold far more danger than night operations and several Bostons became victims of flak. The squadron flew relentlessly attacking rail yards, locomotives and industrial sites. A change of tactics took place in late 1943 when high flying reconnaissance Spitfires took photos of strange ramp-like structures being rapidly built by the enemy along the Channel coast. The Photographic Interpretation Unit at RAF Medmenham identified these as launch ramps for Hitler's long-promised revenge weapon, the V1 or 'Doodlebug'. The sites were code-named 'Noball' sites and from November 1943, the wing at Hartfordbridge was given the job of bombing them.

On the 13th November 1943, the Allied Expeditionary Air Force was born with Air Chief Marshal Sir Trafford Leigh-Mallory as its commander. Sadly it meant the disbandment of Fighter Command two days later for the new command comprised three main components, the American 9th Air Force, the 2nd Tactical Air Force and the Air Defence of Great Britain. All the squadrons at Hartford-bridge joined the new TAF organisation with very little change in operations as 34 Wing continued to photograph the Continent in preparation for the landings.

The Bostons of the Free French now joined No 137 Airfield and continued the bombing of the 'Noball' sites. 107 Squadron moved to Lasham on the 3rd February 1944 and were replaced on the 13th by No 226 who flew their Mitchells in from Swanton Morley in Norfolk. Used primarily as light day-bombers, the main mark of Mitchell used by the RAF was the Mitchell II. Over 500 were delivered under the Lend/Lease agreement and until they were superseded by the more advanced Mosquitos, gave sterling service in the bombing role. Whilst the Mitchells operated from Hartfordbridge, they did not form part of 137 Airfield and carried out independent missions accompanied by the Mitchells stationed at Dunsfold in Surrey.

As the plans for 'Operation Overlord', the allied invasion of Europe, gathered pace, many airfields were visited by the Supreme Allied Commander, General Dwight D Eisenhower. In April 1944 he visited Hartfordbridge and congratulated all the squadrons on doing sterling work in the run-up to D-Day. On the 7th April No 34 Wing comprising Nos 16 and 140 Squadrons moved to Northolt and Spitfires returned to the base in the form of No 322 (Dutch) Squadron. Flying down from Acklington they brought their Mk XIVs for defensive patrols over the south coast of England in order to deter high-flying enemy aircraft from photographing the invasion preparations. Joined in May by No 264 Squadron flying the Mk XIII night-fighter version of the Mosquito, they formed No 141 Airfield. Soon in action, the night of the 14th/15th May saw a flurry of activity for 264 Squadron.

After a period of quiet nights with little enemy activity over England, the Luftwaffe returned in force on these two nights. With the main attack concentrating on Bristol, the Germans lost 11 aircraft in their attempts to flatten the city. Within the bomber force that night was a Junkers JU88 A-2 (1804440), part of No 1 Group of Kampfgeschwader 6. As it approached Bristol it was attacked by a Mosquito of 264 Squadron operating from Hartfordbridge. The aircraft was flown by F/Lt C M Ramsay DFC and F/O Edgar DFC as the navigator. Both saw their cannon shells smash into the Junkers before one of the enemy gunners put a shot into the Mosquito. It proved fatal and as the stricken aircraft pointed its nose downwards, F/Lt Ramsay shouted to his navigator to bale out and then did so himself, but F/O Edgar was killed in the crash. The enemy aircraft broke up over Manor Farm at West Worldham, near Selborne in Hampshire at 2.25 am but not before Oberlt K von Mandwarda (Staffelkapitan) and Oberfw E Frohlich baled out with severe burns and were taken prisoner; Fw H Kaiser, Fw H Wolf and Oberfw P Schmaler were killed. The next night an ME 410 was shot down but with bad weather settling in, it was the last burst of activity for some time to come.

As D-Day approached, the bombing of the French coast continued together with attacks on the V1 sites. The Bostons had been fitted with smoke canisters which were to be used to afford the landing troops some protection from the enemy's eyes. The 6th June arrived and the order was given for the landings to go ahead. By the evening of the 6th, the allies were well established back on European soil.

The success of the landings was made possible by three outstanding factors. The first, the excellent co-ordination of the Allied Air Forces

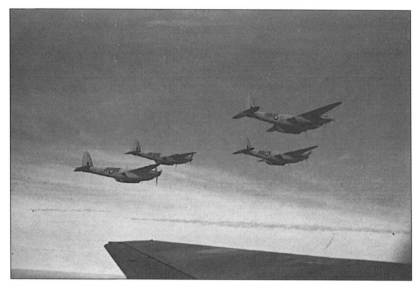

Mosquitos of 605 (County of Warwick) Sqdn, Royal Auxiliary Air Force, airborne from Blackbushe in 1944. (IWM)

who provided an umbrella of aerial protection for the landing troops. The second, the softening-up process by allied bombers on the strategic enemy targets surrounding the landing areas and the third, the superb manoeuvres of the allied forces.

With D-Day a success, No 322 Squadron left for West Malling in Kent and No 141 Wing was disbanded leaving only 214 Squadron to carry on flying night patrols. On the 18th July 1944, Hartfordbridge was honoured to receive King George VI and Queen Elizabeth, who during their visit decorated 80 members of the station.

On the 17th September, one of the greatest of airborne operations took place. Code-named 'Operation Market Garden', it was an attempt to capture the bridges at Nijmegen and Arnhem. In addition an airborne force was also to be dropped at Eindhoven and another at Grave. Air support for this operation was to be provided by No 137 and No 139 Wing and although the weather was not at its best, the Mitchells from Hartfordbridge carried out several daylight raids in advance of the airborne assault. It had been decided that the British would take Arnhem and the Americans the other three targets. As history records, the Americans achieved success but the British, after a tough and very heroic nine-day fight, were forced to surrender before the relieving force could reach them. Unfortunately bad weather had prevented any further flying from Hartfordbridge since the landings had begun, a fact that greatly upset the crews.

The allied troops now fighting on the Continent incurred many casualties and for a period the airfield became a reception centre for troops being flown back to the UK for hospital treatment. The rapid advance into Europe also meant that airfields were now available on the Continent and on the 17th October 1944, No 137 Wing left for Vitry en Artois (B50). No 138 Wing arrived from Lasham but they also moved across the Channel to France. In to Hartfordbridge flew No 136 Mosquito Wing comprising No 418 (City of Edmonton) Canadian Squadron and No 605 (County of Warwick) Squadron. It was also at this time that Hartfordbridge changed its name to Blackbushe.

No 136 Wing operations got under way shortly after Christmas 1944 when Mosquito FB VIs attacked targets ahead of the advancing troops. From the summer of 1944, Mosquito night-fighters were allotted to the Bomber Support Group (No 100 Group). The mark VI was employed in these squadrons in the fighter/bomber role and achieved considerable success whilst with 136 Wing. They too left for the Continent on the 15th March 1945, the last 2nd TAF unit to go to France.

With victory within sight, Blackbushe transferred from the ADGB to No 46 Group Transport Command. In flew No 167 (Gold Coast) Squadron from Holmsley South equipped with Warwick IIIs. A development of the Vickers Warwick I transport, the mark III was available as a VIP transport with seating for eight to ten passengers or for ordinary trooping duties with 24 men and equipment. A total of 100 aircraft were built before production ceased in October 1945. 167 Squadron operated freight and passenger services to and from the Continent and were joined by No 301 (Pomeranian) Polish Squadron who converted from Liberators to Warwicks whilst at Blackbushe.

A glimpse of the future use of the airfield came during the same month when No 167 Squadron added regular flights to the Channel Islands as part of their duties. Now free from Nazi tyranny, the islands were getting back to normal and the flights by 167 were the forerunners to the commencement of civilian services to Jersey and Guernsey. They used Ansons for the purpose and with the arrival of No 162 Squadron from Bourne on the 6th July 1945, Blackbushe was once again a very busy airfield.

No 162 Squadron flew the Mosquito XX but not really in a military

Blackbushe airport in 1974. The wartime watch office/control tower is clearly seen on the end of the hangar. (L Pilkington)

role. They were used for express delivery services to countries such as Egypt, Italy and Greece where British troops were still stationed. Later on Gibraltar and Malta were added to the list but with the ending of the war, it soon became obvious that civilian airlines would be taking over some of these duties.

Sure enough, in 1946, the newly formed British European Airways took over the duties of 167 Squadron and they disbanded at Blackbushe. The airfield began to take on a commercial role as Danish Airlines commenced scheduled services to Copenhagen and Stockholm on the 6th September. 1946 also saw No 160 Staging Post installed and carrying out ferry and VIP flights but the end of the military presence at Blackbushe was in sight as No 162 Squadron disbanded on the 14th July 1946. RAF Blackbushe officially closed on the 15th November 1946 after 11,444 aircraft and 63,934 passengers had passed through the terminal since its changeover to Transport Command in February 1945. It passed to the Ministry of Civil Aviation who re-opened it on the 15th February 1947 as Blackbushe Airport.

5
CHATTIS HILL

If ever natural camouflage worked to its best advantage it was at Chattis Hill, situated $2\frac{1}{2}$ miles west of Stockbridge. After its use as a 1914/18 war base, it was abandoned and reverted back to natural countryside. For the next 20 years the grass was trodden down by horses' hoofs as it became a popular exercise area for racehorses. When the site was resurrected in December 1940 for the second conflict, the tracks made by the horses had the appearance of an area that was nothing but a series of fields and ditches. From the air, Chattis Hill did not resemble an airfield at all yet it gave sterling service as a dispersal and production centre for Spitfires.

Thursday 26th September 1940 dawned mainly fair with a little high cloud in the south. For several days there had been sporadic attacks on the Supermarine works at Woolston near Southampton. German reconnaissance photos had showed that these attacks had not really hit the main factory and it was decided that an all-out effort by the Luftwaffe against Woolston would be carried out early in the afternoon of the 26th. The task was given to Kampfgeschwader 55 stationed at Villaboublay under the command of Oberst Alois Stocki. Crossing the English coastline they made straight for the Supermarine plants at Woolston and the recently completed plant at Itchen and carried out a devastating raid. Fifty-nine Heinkel 111s delivered a precise bombing attack dropping over 70 tons of bombs. Both works were wrecked but even more tragic was the 30 lives lost. Immediately after the attack the site was visited by Lord Beaverbrook, the minister for aircraft production who ordered that the two factories were to be abandoned and that the production operation should be dispersed to less obvious

A Heinkel HE111 of KG53 runs up its engines prior to an assault on Britain. (Bundesarchiv)

sites. Chattis Hill was perfect for such use and the site was resurrected once again.

Prepared during the summer of 1917, the first unit to use the grass airfield was No 91 (Nigerian) Squadron who formed at Chattis Hill on the 1st September 1917. The squadron was engaged in wireless telegraphy training with an assortment of aircraft until it disbanded on the 4th July 1918. No 93 Squadron formed at the same time as 91 but was a fighter unit equipped with SE 5As. It saw no action and was disbanded in October 1918. The aircraft were hangared in Bessoneaux hangars and the personnel lived in tented accommodation. Bad weather usually brought the airfield to a halt as the grass became mud, making conditions unbearable. This only improved when an American construction unit arrived in 1918 to build a more permanent station. When completed the airfield was used as a storage field for aircraft before being abandoned in 1920. It remained this way for 20 years until the devastating blow by the Luftwaffe on the Supermarine works gave it a new lease of life.

Immediately after the raid, Chattis Hill was operational. Jigs and machine tools were brought over from Woolston and production began. With the hangars built around the perimeter in the shelter of the trees, it was the perfect camouflage. The airfield was used for the final erection and test flying of Spitfires and the finished product was flown out of Chattis Hill by pilots of the Air Transport Auxiliary based at Hamble.

Whilst the Solent area was subjected to several more large raids, by the end of September the enemy forsook his attacks on Fighter Command and the aircraft manufacturing plants at the expense of the blitz on London. Although this eventually meant a resumption of work at Woolston, assembly of the Spitfire continued at Chattis Hill until the end of the war. There is no doubt that without the availability of airfields such as Chattis Hill, Spitfire production would have suffered dearly with very uncertain consequences for the outcome of the aerial battle. With the help of this site and other dispersal airfields around the Hampshire area, the figures for the overall picture of Spitfire production during the last months of 1940 were 136 in September, 149 in October, 139 in November and 117 in December.

When the war ended all flying ceased but further Spitfire parts were still manufactured until May 1948 when the site closed. Chattis Hill returned to nature, the assembly sheds were removed and little can be seen today to remind us of a very important dispersal and production site for the Supermarine Spitfire.

6
CHILBOLTON

Work began here in 1939 on levelling 145 acres of land belonging to Manor Farm, one mile south of Chilbolton village. With the bomber base of Middle Wallop just a few miles away, Chilbolton was intended to be a dispersal and satellite airfield. By the time it was completed however, Middle Wallop had become operational as a Fighter Command base and with four squadrons in residence, was becoming rather overcrowded. To ease the situation, No 238 Squadron equipped with Hurricane Is flew the short distance to Chilbolton on the 30th September 1940. Arriving in the morning, the squadron went into action at noon as 40 Heinkel bombers escorted by fighters crossed the English coastline and headed for the Westland works at Yeovil. In heavy cloud, two of the Hurricanes of 238 Squadron collided. L1702 crashed near Shaftesbury just after 2 pm. The pilot, P/O R A Kings managed to bale out but as his parachute was damaged as he left his aircraft, he was injured in a heavy landing. Hurricane N2474 flown by P/O V C Simmonds was also a write-off but once again, he managed to bale out and landed safely. No contact was made by the squadron with the enemy due to the poor weather conditions.

The next day tragedy struck again as a large force of German aircraft attempted to bomb Southampton and Portsmouth. Led by the Messerschmitt Bf 110s of Lehrgeschwader 1 operating from Caen, the main bomber force comprised aircraft from KG 30, KG 51 and KG 53. Over the target area they met stiff opposition and in the ensuing fight, Hurricane P3599 was shot down over Poole Harbour at 11.10 am; the pilot Sgt F A Sidley was never found. In the same action, another Hurricane R4099 was also shot down over Poole but P/O A R

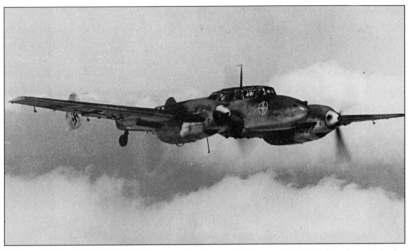

Messerschmitt ME110-3. Used extensively as a fighter and fighter/bomber, it had a distinguished career in the Luftwaffe. (MAP)

Covington baled out and landed to fight another day.

No 238 were not back in action until Saturday 5th October 1940 when they were scrambled from Chilbolton to deal with a large force of ME 109s carrying bombs and heading for Southampton once again. Approaching Shaftesbury a dogfight developed and S/Ldr J R MacLauchlan was shot down. Managing to bale out from his blazing Hurricane, (P3611) he was admitted to Shaftesbury Hospital with burns. The enemy also suffered badly having lost 26 aircraft, but at sunset Fighter Command noted that 1,175 sorties had been flown on just that one day.

As winter approached the German raids became fewer but No 238 continued to take further losses. By the end of the Battle of Britain, deemed to be Thursday 31st October 1940, they had lost 17 Hurricanes.

No 238 Squadron remained at Chilbolton until January 1941 when they returned to Middle Wallop. The 1st February 1941 saw them back and converting to the Hurricane IIA before departing to Pembrey on the 1st April.

In 1940, many of the Allied-manned squadrons were adopting the names of their cities and incorporating them in the official squadron titles. One such squadron manned by Polish personnel was No 308 (Krakow) who arrived at Chilbolton on the 31st May 1941 with their

Spitfire Is, quickly converting to the mark IIA. They only flew a few sorties before going on to Northolt and were in turn replaced by No 501 (County of Gloucester) Squadron of the Royal Auxiliary Air Force. They had recently converted to the Spitfire IIA and began carrying out offensive sweeps over the French mainland. Known as 'Rhubarbs', a code name for low-level strike operations against targets in occupied Europe, they stayed for less than a month and flew to Ibsley on the 5th August.

Another brief appearance came in the form of No 504 (County of Nottingham) Auxiliary Squadron who brought their Hurricane IIBs in from Fairwood Common and left 15 days later for Ballyhalbert in Ireland. In this period of rapid changes, No 245 (Northern Rhodesia) Squadron came to Chilbolton a month later and commenced offensive operations with their Hurricane IIBs. Their motto 'I put to flight, I do not flee' was very apt as they carried out shipping strikes on the French and Belgian ports.

As with many of the early wartime airfields, Chilbolton was a grass airfield. This led to problems of waterlogging etc and although the laying of Sommerfeld Tracking helped the situation in many cases, some grass even made this buckle and distort. Although Chilbolton was upgraded in late 1941, Sommerfeld was not laid but the airfield did get a concrete perimeter track and some aircraft hard-standings. During the rebuild, no permanent squadrons were based there although it was used as an Army Relief Landing Ground. In November 1942, Chilbolton was reduced to care and maintenance but on the 7th December, it became a satellite to Netheravon indicating its use by the Army.

By Christmas 1942, the De Havilland Tiger Moths of the Glider Pilots Exercise Unit had arrived and the airfield had transferred to No 38 Wing. By 1943 all eyes were on an invasion of the European mainland by the Allies and part of the pre-invasion exercises involved the Army at Chilbolton. Exercise 'Spartan' was held over February/March 1943 and it involved a detachment to the airfield of No 174 (Mauritius) Squadron with Hurricane IIBs and No 184 Squadron with the Hurricane IID, the latter being a tank busting version of the famous fighter equipped with two 40 mm Vickers 'S' guns. The exercise jointly carried out by the Army and the RAF was a great success and the squadrons remained at Chilbolton for 11 days before moving on to Grove.

Transferred to No 70 Group on the 21st April 1943, another

upgrading was carried out but still Chilbolton remained a grass airfield. More land was acquired as the domestic and landing areas were extended and extra hangarage in the shape of two T2 sheds indicated a new use for the airfield.

Chilbolton returned to No 10 Group Fighter Command on the 1st June, but it was not until December that a new unit arrived in the form of the 5th Tactical Air Depot joined later by the 68th Fighter Group from Greenham Common in March 1944. Chilbolton had been taken over by the 9th Air Force of the USAAF.

If ever a need arose for a concrete runway it was during this period of Chilbolton's war as the heavy P47 Thunderbolts of the 395th, 396th and 397th Fighter Squadrons continually ripped up the grass. When it rained the poor drainage allowed the water to sit on top of the grass and many Thunderbolts took off or landed covered in mud!

On the 6th June 1944 in the greatest combined operation of all time, the Allies assaulted the strongly fortified coast of France. As a softening-up process, the Thunderbolts from Chilbolton attacked airfields, industry, bridges and in fact anything that would hinder the enemy's chance of retaliation. In addition they attacked the 'Noball' V1 rocket sites in Northern France, with single bombs as well as with guns. As the Allies got a foothold in France, the pressure was kept up and dawn to dusk operations were the order of the day at Chilbolton. By the 19th June it was all over and when it moved from Chilbolton, the 368th Fighter Group was to gain the distinction of being the first USAAF fighter group to operate from an advance air base in newly liberated France. The local residents breathed a sigh of relief for there was no doubt that this period had been one of the busiest and the noisiest in the airfield's history. Although still a grass airfield, Chilbolton saw a new use as the USAAF flew in their wounded en route to a temporary hospital at Stockbridge. Transport aircraft of the 442nd Troop Carrier Group moved in on the 11th September and began supply flights to the advancing allied troops in Normandy. Six days later 45 C47 Dakotas took off from Chilbolton carrying the airborne troops for the invasion of Holland. Code-named 'Operation Market Garden', it had all the ingredients for success yet it proved to be a sad failure. It took place on Sunday 17th September under a cover of 1,200 allied aircraft yet at the final tally, over 3,700 American airborne personnel and a total of around 11,000 men of all the other units were either killed, wounded or posted as missing. Several misfortunes caused the failure of 'Market Garden' including the fact that full details of the operation were found by the Germans on the body of an American officer killed in a glider accident over enemy lines. Thus heavy artillery was moved into the area making capture of the area much more difficult. Another cause was the breakdown of communication equipment, possibly due to the lack of maintenance and training. These and other factors were responsible for a great tragedy.

The operation over, Chilbolton was returned to the RAF in March 1945 when an operational training unit arrived with a selection of aircraft including Hurricanes, Spitfires and Martinets. Regraded as a forward airfield in the Middle Wallop sector of No 11 Group, No 26 (South African) Squadron flew their Mustang Is in from Harrowbeer in Scotland on the 23rd May 1945. Converting to the Spitfire XIV in June, they were joined by No 183 (Gold Coast) Squadron bringing a new type of aircraft to Chilbolton in the shape of the Typhoon IB. They converted to the Spitfire IX later and the two squadrons carried out exercises until the 20th August 1945 when No 26 moved to the Continent to B 164/Schleswig airfield. No 183 remained until the 8th October before going to Fairwood Common but they were back at Chilbolton on the 15th November with the Tempest II. The same day they disbanded and were renumbered No 54 Squadron, remaining at Chilbolton until June 1946 when they moved over to Odiham to go jet-powered with the De Havilland Vampire F1.

This same aircraft first flew at Chilbolton in March 1946 when No 247 (China-British) Squadron became the first squadron to fly the Vampire in front-line service. Arriving on the 16th February 1946 with Tempest F2s, the conversion took place shortly after concrete runways had been laid in preparation for the first jet aircraft. On the 8th June, 247 were honoured to fly the type in the Victory Day fly-past over London and together with Nos 54 and 72 (Basutoland) Squadrons, formed Fighter Command's first Vampire wing. They departed to West Malling in Kent on the 1st June 1946 returning for 15 days on the 12th June. When they left, Chilbolton was once again returned to care and maintenance but was about to embark on a new career of experimental and test flying.

7
EASTLEIGH
(SOUTHAMPTON)

The Air Ministry specification F.7/30 started the entire Spitfire story. This led to Supermarine issuing their own specification No F.37/34 dated 3rd January 1935 which called for an experimental high speed single-seat fighter. In March 1936, the prototype s/n K5054 was cleared to begin flight trials. Captain J 'Mutt' Summers went to Eastleigh to fly the first flight and it was here that the ultimate success of the Spitfire began.

Situated $1\frac{1}{2}$ miles south of Eastleigh town, the site was used for experimental flying before the First World War. Used briefly by Grahame White, one of the very early pioneers of powered flight, it fell out of use around 1912 until the RFC depot in Leigh Road decided to expand in 1917. Four hangars and several sheds were built and the airfield became an Aircraft Acceptance Park. In April 1918, the US Navy were looking for sites in the UK and decided that Eastleigh was an ideal base for bomber aircraft. Commissioned as Naval Air Station Eastleigh, on the 23rd July 1918, the armistice was agreed before any real use could be made of it. The navy left in April 1919 and the airfield was handed back to the RAF.

The 1920s saw the rise of a remarkable man called Alan Cobham. One of his ambitions was to make Britain air-minded and in order to achieve this he had two plans. One was his municipal aerodrome campaign and the other was National Aviation Day campaign. Flying a De Havilland DH61 which he had christened 'Youth of Britain', he commenced the first of several exhausting tours that would eventually

Early Eastleigh days with a Jersey Airways Dragon Rapide beside the hangars. (L Pilkington)

bring him to Southampton and to Eastleigh airfield.

Arriving on the 11th August 1932, Alan Cobham was met by the mayor, town clerk and the entire council committee. Discussions were held as to the feasibility of a municipal aerodrome for Southampton and after lunch, local dignitaries were flown in the DH61. So impressed was the council with the presentation that the corporation purchased 100 acres of land belonging to the old airfield and work commenced on a civil municipal airport.

Eastleigh was officially opened in November 1932 and at the same time, Supermarine had approached the council with a view to using the field for flight testing. With negotiations concluded between the council and the Royal Aircraft Establishment, Supermarine established a facility at Eastleigh, beginning a long period of association with the area.

The airfield attracted flying clubs, Jersey Airways commenced civil flying from the site and in May 1935, Railway Air Services included it in their ever-increasing network of routes. The site became known as Southampton Airport, and an agreement between the civil authorities and the Air Ministry enabled many RAF squadrons to hold summer camps on the field as further negotiations saw the establishment of an

The Speed Spitfire was built for an attempt on the World Land-plane Speed Record in 1937. It took the honour but was overtaken later by a German Heinkel 100. It later served in a photographic unit of the RAF. (Flight)

FAA unit in the north-east corner of the airfield. Canvas Bessoneaux hangars and accommodation were erected in time for No 802 Squadron FAA to fly their Nimrods in for a few weeks before embarking on *HMS Glorious*.

With the international situation deteriorating rapidly, it became obvious that Britain lacked a modern credible fighter. Supermarine with their test facility at Southampton were working on a single seat aircraft and as already stated, the first prototype Spitfire K5054 was flown from Southampton.

On the 3rd June 1936 the Air Ministry placed an order for 310 Spitfires but as Supermarine was also building the Walrus and Stranraer flying boats in nearby assembly plants in addition to their Southampton Spitfire assembly plant, it became obvious that some of the work would have to be sub-contracted. Meanwhile test flying continued but though the war clouds loomed over Europe, the first production Spitfire, K9787, was not ready to fly until the 15th May 1938.

The key Woolston factory for Spitfire production after it was attacked. (Crown copyright)

The trials from Southampton were not without their problems. Modifications had to be done after each series of flight tests and so it was the 19th July 1938 before the RAF received its first production Spitfire, K9798. By the beginning of 1939, 49 aircraft had been delivered but delivery was by no means fast enough. Although the Hawker Hurricane was being delivered to the RAF in greater numbers, it became obvious that, compared to the Luftwaffe, Fighter Command would be grossly under-equipped.

In May 1937 the airfield was used by aircraft taking part in the Spithead Review and Empire Air Day which that year attracted a vast crowd, all eager to see the new aircraft that were coming into service. A detachment of No 22 Squadron brought their Vildebeestes for a stay followed by No 42 Squadron who also sent detachments to Lee-on-Solent, Gosport and Tangmere. Both squadrons left in March 1938 as did Nos 264 and 269 Squadrons who had flown Ansons from the field from January to March.

As the clouds of war gathered, the Air Ministry became responsible for air traffic facilities in April 1938. Civil aircraft continued to use Southampton and a new aircraft manufacturing company, Cuncliffe-Owen Aircraft Ltd had established a factory on the airfield to promote the Burnelli Flying Wing, a somewhat futuristic aircraft. When they moved to a different location in January 1939, the ever-expanding

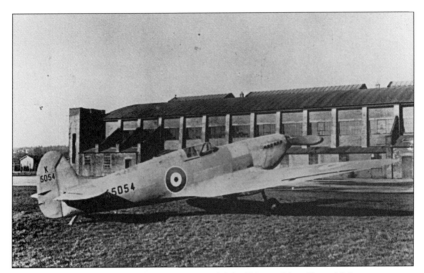

The first production Spitfire K5054 at Eastleigh. (Hampshire Chronicle)

Supermarine took over their hangar. As if with forethought, the Prime Minister, Mr Neville Chamberlain, stated on the 28th January 1939, 'We cannot forget that though it takes at least two to make peace, one can make a war and until we have come to a clear understanding, we must put ourselves in a position to defend ourselves. Our motto,' he said, 'is not defiance, it is not either deference. It is defence'.

In preparation for the expected onslaught, civil flying ceased at Southampton and the FAA was transferred from RAF to RN charge on the 24th May. On the 1st July, Southampton became HMS Raven of the FAA. That same day, No 758 Squadron was formed as a telegraphist air gunner Training Squadron within No 2 Air Gunners School which was commanded by L/C W H G Saunt. It was initially equipped with 13 Siskins and six Ospreys with the addition of Skuas and Proctors during 1940. Also forming at the airfield on the 1st November 1939 was No 759 Squadron. This was a fighter school and pool squadron equipped initially with nine Skuas, five Rocs and four Sea Gladiators. Commanded by L/C B H M Kendall, 759 did sterling work in the training of FAA pilots.

By the eve of war, all the buildings had been camouflaged, shelters had been dug and the army defences were in place. It was a period of rapid changes for the FAA and a great variety of aircraft were flying in

Another shot of the first of the many at Eastleigh, 1937. (Crown copyright)

and out of HMS Raven. No 760 Squadron formed at the airfield on the 1st April 1940 as Fleet Fighter Pool No 1. Once again the aircraft consisted of Skuas, Rocs and Sea Gladiators.

With the Battle of Britain raging overhead, only one RAF squadron was ever based at HMS Raven during this period. No 266 (Rhodesia) Squadron equipped with Spitfire Is arrived on the 12th August for a stay of two days before going on to Hornchurch in Essex.

During the third phase of the battle, considered to have run from 24th August to 6th September, the full terror of war was brought to the airfield. During this period Fighter Command was near breaking point.

Cloudy weather from the 19th August to the 23rd gave a lull in the enemy attacks. It also gave time for the Luftwaffe to adjust its tactics. It appeared to the senior commanders that Fighter Command had not been fully brought into the battle and that if an invasion of Britain was to be attempted, the RAF must be cleared from the skies as well as pinned down on the ground. Goering therefore issued a new directive on the 19th August stating 'to continue the fight against the enemy air force until further notice, with the aim of weakening the British fighter forces. The enemy is to be forced to use his fighters by means of ceaseless attacks. In addition the aircraft industry and the ground

Spitfires undergoing assembly at Eastleigh. (Flight)

organisation of the air force are to be attacked by means of individual aircraft by night and day, if weather conditions do not permit the use of complete formations'.

Saturday 24th August therefore saw the battle enter a new phase of tactics. With the early part of Saturday morning fine and cloudless, the controllers at 11 Group headquarters and the radar stations on the coast waited for the first formations to form up over France. They did not have to wait long. At 9 am, German aircraft were plotted crossing the French coast. Aircraft from Fliegerkorps II operating from Arras, Epinoy and Cambrai crossed the Channel and attacked Dover and the fighter airfield of Manston. Further raids during the day left Manston virtually isolated from all communications but it was shortly after 2 pm that Junkers 88s and Heinkel 111s of Luftflotte 3 attacked Portsmouth and Southampton. The raid caused considerable damage in the town but Eastleigh survived with just one stick of bombs being dropped on the southern perimeter. (Although now known as Southampton Airport, the military still referred to the site as Eastleigh.) The enemy suffered badly as 15 squadrons of Fighter Command attacked them. At Eastleigh, the naval ratings looked upwards as a ME 109 pursued by a

Part of the Hampshire Regiment was briefed to man the airfield defences at Eastleigh/ Southampton airfield during the Battle of Britain. (Mrs P Elliot)

Hurricane raced across the airfield. In a flash the German had been hit and as the stricken aircraft crossed the coast and began to lose height, the pilot Fw G Ebus bailed out. The aircraft crashed on Shanklin Down on the Isle of Wight but the pilot fell into the sea and drowned. His body was pulled from the sea at Ventnor by a naval launch and he was buried at St Ann's Hill cemetery, Gosport where he remains to this day.

During this one day the Luftwaffe flew 1,030 sorties and lost 38 fighters and bombers. Fighter Command on the other hand flew 936 sorties and lost 22 fighters. Though it appeared that the RAF was faring better than the Luftwaffe in losses, the enemy had far more aircraft in reserve than they did.

The next day, Sunday, saw little enemy activity until 5 pm when 180 enemy aircraft approached the Portland area. With several fighter squadrons scrambled, the German raiders were intercepted in good time and very little damage was caused to the towns around Portland. All of this changed on the Monday when at 4 pm, a major raid approached Portsmouth along a 30 mile front. KG 55 operating from Villacoublay, Dreux and Chartres attempted to bomb Portsmouth and Southampton, once again from a high altitude. In response, No 11

Early MkI Spitfires at Eastleigh. (Flight)

Group scrambled five squadrons whilst No 10 Group scrambled three. Intercepting the Heinkel 111s over the sea, the fighters managed to destroy three of the enemy aircraft causing many of the others to jettison their bombs into the sea and head for home. Although all of this could be seen from Eastleigh, no damage was done to the airfield.

The rest of August and early September carried on in similar manner but the spirited defiance put up by Fighter Command continued to puzzle and annoy the Luftwaffe commanders. If they had known the truth, that the RAF was actually fighting a losing battle due to a lack of pilots, the outcome may well have been different. As it was, 'Operation Sealion', the planned invasion of Britain, was postponed by Hitler from Wednesday 11th September 1940 until at least the 14th of the month. Whether it went ahead on that date would depend on the RAF being driven from the skies and in another attempt to draw the fighters up, the 11th September saw heavy raids over Hampshire.

The morning began with heavy jamming of the Chain Home and Chain Home Low radar stations. Ventnor radar was very confused from early morning and was one of the stations attacked during the morning. During the afternoon Luftflotte 5 was scheduled to attack Southampton and in particular Eastleigh airfield. The Heinkel 111s of KG 26 flying from Stavanger in Norway came in and dropped their bombs on the works of Cuncliffe-Owen. So much damage was caused by this raid that it was decided to vacate the airfield. Nos 759 and 760

Crew members of a Heinkel HE111 of KG26 relax before a bombing mission over England. Unlike their British counterparts, they flew mostly from grass airfields. (Bundesarchiv)

Squadrons of the FAA left on the 16th September followed by No 780 on the 7th October and No 758 on the 14th. Eastleigh was now left to Cuncliffe-Owen.

Although the airfield lay almost deserted, this did not stop the Luftwaffe thinking that it was of great importance. The next sizeable raid took place on the 15th October when bombs were dropped but with most of the Spitfire production and test flying being done at the dispersal sites such as Chattis Hill, the raid did not interrupt the war effort. It did however ensure that no more Spitfire test flying was done from Eastleigh.

Although now deprived of naval aircraft the airfield remained as HMS Raven and became a training base. October 1940 saw the Battle of Britain peter out as the darker nights of autumn arrived and as history tells us, all thoughts of an invasion of Britain were postponed for about a year. It was now the period of night bombing on the cities. At the same time the pressure on the airfields relented by day and it was the turn of the night-fighters to deal with the enemy.

1941 saw many cities suffer from the indiscriminate bombing by the

Messerschmitt BF109-G – the mainstay of the Luftwaffe fighter force. (MAP)

Luftwaffe but at Eastleigh a new manufacturing plant had been set up at the factory of Cuncliffe-Owen. They had previously been involved in the repair and modification of various types of aircraft but in 1941, a decision was taken by the Air Ministry to modify certain land-based aircraft for carrier borne operations. One of these conversions involved the Spitfire which had already undertaken deck landing trials aboard *HMS Illustrious*. In late 1941, work went ahead to convert some Spitfires into Seafires and a contract was awarded to Cuncliffe-Owen for part of the production. Called Seafire IBs, about 48 were built and tested at Eastleigh and the type entered first line service with No 807 Squadron in June 1942. Production of the Seafire III was undertaken at Eastleigh by Cuncliffe-Owen and at Yeovil by Westland. Out of a total of 1,220 aircraft, the former company built 350 between November 1943 and July 1945. In 1944, Cuncliffe-Owen also built and tested 134 Griffon engined Seafires, the mark XV. This aircraft eventually entered service with the FAA when the war came to an end. Later marks of the Seafire were also built and tested at Eastleigh by Cuncliffe-Owen including a carrier-borne version of the powerful Spitfire 21.

Meanwhile, the airfield had also become home to the Air Medicine School and the Safety Equipment School of the Royal Navy. Once again naval aircraft such as Barracudas were flying from Eastleigh and they

Spitfires at the assembly plant. After the Woolston factory was bombed on 26th September 1940, production of parts was dispersed to several sites. (Soton Hall of Aviation)

were joined in September 1945 by the Dragon Rapides of Channel Island Airways who re-opened the civilian link with Jersey and Guernsey.

Eastleigh remained as HMS Raven until April 1946 when the navy relinquished the airfield and the Ministry of Civil Aviation took it over. The name Eastleigh reverted back to Southampton (Eastleigh) Airport and the association with scheduled and charter services began once again.

8
FARNBOROUGH

The story of Farnborough airfield begins in the era of balloons in 1905 when the Royal Engineers started a balloon factory, later known as the Balloon School, at the northern end of Farnborough Common. There they built the army's first dirigible and later completed larger airships such as the Beta, Gamma and Delta. The arrival of Samuel Franklin Cody in February 1905 brought the first powered aircraft to Farnborough and in 1908, it was Cody who made the first sustained aeroplane flight in the British Isles. The first of many flying pioneers had arrived at Farnborough.

The birth of the RFC on the 13th May 1912 saw the first military aircraft at the airfield. No 4 Squadron was formed equipped with BE 2cs and moved to Netheravon on the 14th June 1913. With the outbreak of war in 1914, most of the RFC squadrons moved to France and throughout the duration of the First World War, Farnborough was an RFC depot, the Records Office and the home of the Reserve Aeroplane Squadrons. At the end of the war and upon the formation of the RAF Farnborough was renamed the Royal Aircraft Establishment and in 1921 it absorbed the Instrument Design Establishment from Biggin Hill and the Air Worthiness Department of the Air Ministry.

The facilities required by the RAE were enormous. With the testing and research work to be done on aircraft, engines, flight refuelling procedures and high altitude flight among other tasks, it was essential that no expense was spared in making Farnborough a place of excellence. Wind tunnels and a huge seaplane test tank were constructed. New altitude records were set by aircraft flying from Farnborough but with the prospect of another war with Germany imminent, the station was transferred to No 24 Group on the 10th July 1936. No 4 Squadron, who had been flying Audax aircraft from the airfield, left on the 16th February 1937 and were replaced by No 53 Squadron who reformed at Farnborough on the 28th June 1937. Formed as an Army Co-operation Unit, they flew Hawker Hectors and specialised in night reconnaissance. This aircraft was the replacement for the Hawker Audax and had the uprated Napier Dagger engine in place of the less powerful Rolls Royce Kestrel. They left to join the Odiham wing a year later and Farnborough became home to No 1 Anti-Aircraft Co-op Unit flying the Westland Wallace.

Reverting to No 22 Group Control in 1938, the airfield was used by further anti-aircraft units and the School of Photography as the war loomed closer. Despite all the extra units that had been sent to Farnborough, the RAF still carried on with its experimental tasks. Even the outbreak of war at 11 am on Sunday 3rd September 1939 did not stop the work on evaluating new aircraft and systems.

It was however not only British aircraft that were to be taken to Farnborough for this process. As far back as 1938 it was intended that the RAE would be the establishment that would test and evaluate enemy aircraft as well. One of the first to receive the attention of the 'boffins' was a ME 109E which had landed at Rimling near Sarreguehines in the Moselle area of France on the 24th September 1939. Known as Black 9, it belonged to the 2nd Gruppe of JG 77. It was inspected by the RAF at Nancy on the 3rd October, damaged in a later flight, repaired and flown to Britain to be first taken to Boscombe Down. From here it was transported to Farnborough and flown on many occasions with RAF markings. It was the first of many that the RAE flew in the process of evaluation.

Obviously a research and experimental establishment soon came to the attention of the enemy. Friday 2nd August dawned cloudy with a little drizzle in the Dover Straits, hampering the enemy who was only able to mount an attack on an east coast convoy. By nightfall the cloud had gone and it became a clear night. Over 80 mine-laying HE 111s were plotted from the Orkneys to Dungeness and between the hours of 10.45 pm and 2 am, 65 high explosive bombs were dropped by the Luftwaffe. The main targets were the RAF Technical College at Halton and the airfields of Catterick and Farnborough. At the latter the damage was minimal and no one was killed but it did indicate that the enemy knew where and what the purpose of the airfield was.

The next raid intended for Farnborough was on Tuesday 13th

The mainstay of the Luftwaffe bomber fleet – the Heinkel 111. (MAP)

August. Known to the Luftwaffe as 'Adler Tag' (Eagle Day), it marked an increase in enemy activity in the hope of neutralising the airfields of Fighter Command and clearing the RAF from the skies for a September invasion. For these opening attacks Luftflotten 2 and 3 were ready for the battle. It fell to KG 54, commanded by Oberst Hohne to attack Odiham airfield and the RAE at Farnborough, but with low cloud persisting in the early morning, it was not until 11 am that the bombers were airborne. Even then the attack did not go smoothly for at the last moment a signal from the Reichsmarschall postponed 'Adler Tag' until the afternoon. Three units however, including KG 54, did not get the signal and the JU 88s continued to head for the English coastline. Crossing the coast they broke into two sections escorted by fighters but the radar stations had plotted them and they were engaged over the coast by No 43 Squadron operating from Tangmere. They ploughed into the enemy formations; the first to fall was a JU 88 which crashed and exploded in Swanbourne Lake near Arundel. A second one was shot down over Trayford and, severely damaged, several others turned and headed for home. Joined by Nos 601 and 64 Squadrons the Spitfires of all three squadrons pressed home their attacks so ferociously that the Luftwaffe missed their targets and Farnborough remained unscathed.

And so 'Adler Tag' passed but it was not the day the enemy had hoped for. This did not however deter the Luftwaffe from mounting further large raids, by day and by night. Friday 16th August 1940 was a typical hot summer's day. In the morning it was the turn of Norfolk, Kent and the Greater London area to be bombed and in the evening, the raids concentrated on Portland and Farnborough airfield. Once again the aircraft of Luftflotte 2 and 3, their crews weary from previous sorties, crossed the coastline at night and dropped their bombs, unhampered by British fighters. At Farnborough, 8 JU 88s came in low and dropped 20 HE bombs on the RAE. Warned of the approach of enemy aircraft, most of the men and women were in the underground shelters but the impact of some of the bombs was sufficient to penetrate one shelter. Three people lost their lives and several more were injured. As ambulances sped to the scene of the disaster, the men and women were emerging from the shelters to see what they could of the devastation. Many began pulling bricks and rubble away from the crushed shelter in an effort to reach the dead and the injured. The business of the RAE was badly disrupted for several days but slowly the airfield returned to normality. In a summary of the operations so far it was stated by the Luftwaffe high command that 372 Spitfires, 179 Hurricanes, 9 Curtiss Hawks and 12 Defiants had been destroyed in the period from the 1st July to the 15th August 1940. It was further stated in a letter to Hitler himself that Fighter Command now only possessed 300 serviceable aircraft. In actual fact the command had over 700 aircraft. It was however the lack of trained pilots that mainly worried Dowding. For some time he had been pressing for Fairey Battle pilots to fill the gap but the Air Ministry declined. At Farnborough, the Experimental Flying Department took their own decision and formed a station defence flight with a Spitfire, two Hurricanes and a Gladiator. Such was the spirit of the RAE in the face of danger.

The rest of August was given to major attacks on the airfields although Farnborough was not the subject of attention. By the beginning of November, the Battle of Britain was over but the work of the RAE continued, including work on gyro gun sights, bomb aiming equipment and of course, future aircraft development. Very little is known even today of just what secret work was carried out at the airfield.

It was 1942 before another squadron became resident at Farnborough. No 653 (AOP) Squadron brought their Tiger Moths across from Old Sarum on the 8th July. They converted first to the Taylorcraft Plus C2 whilst at Farnborough and then in August to the Auster I. Part of

An Avro Anson C19 seen at Farnborough post-war. Earlier marks of this aircraft were the norm on many airfields in Hampshire. (MAP)

the 2nd TAF, the Austers proved very successful in the role of artillery spotting. They were built by Taylorcraft Aeroplanes (England) Ltd, who later became Auster Aircraft Ltd. 653 Squadron received 20 of these at Farnborough before moving to Penshurst in Kent on the 7th September 1942.

Returning to No 24 Group control in October 1943, the airfield saw detachments of anti-aircraft co-operative units arrive and depart frequently. These provided aircraft for use with the army and naval anti-aircraft guns situated around the country. On the other side of the airfield it was business as usual for the RAE with work on high speed flight trials. As aircraft got progressively faster and new and more powerful engines were built, the effects on both man and machine were tested to the full at Farnborough. With no further attacks, the airfield saw the end of the war out in relative quiet.

Since 1984, when Farnborough survived closure, the SBAC airshows have become known as the shop window for British aviation. Cody's first flight is remembered by a commemorative plaque attached to what is known as Cody's Tree. Though not open on a public basis, the RAE museum reminds us all of the superb work done by this establishment over the years. Now sadly, Farnborough is once again threatened with closure but with another public outcry it may yet survive.

9
GOSPORT

Unlike its neighbour, Sussex, Hampshire has always seen the Fleet Air Arm very prominent within its borders. With the naval base at Portsmouth, it became necessary to build shore based airfields to deploy aircraft from the carriers that used the port. Training establishments were needed between the wars to further naval aviation and although not a fighter station, Gosport filled the role admirably and received a lot of attention from the Luftwaffe for this reason.

Gosport came about during the expansion period of the RFC during 1912 and was situated four miles west of Portsmouth in an area known as Grange Camp Field. With most of the RFC units forming part of the British Expeditionary Force, 1914 saw the majority of them cross the water to France. It was the formation of two RNAS squadrons that really gave birth to Gosport and its long association with naval aviation. With the erection of canvas hangars and tented accommodation for the personnel, the airfield prepared for action but because of a dispute between the Admiralty and the War Office, it was the RFC that arrived in the form of No 8 Squadron on the 6th January 1915. Four days later No 13 Squadron formed at Gosport and on the 1st February 1915, No 17 followed a similar pattern. All three squadrons formed the 5th Wing equipped with BE 2cs and were at Gosport for training purposes. Further expansion of the airfield took place during 1915 when No 22 Squadron formed from a nucleus of No 13 Squadron with Longhorns. No 23 followed a similar path but once again, most of the squadrons moved over to France in due course.

With the formation of the RAF in 1918, Gosport became part of No 2 area parented by No 8 Group in Southampton. HQ Gosport was formed on the 28th October 1918 to manage a special experimental flight together with several research units but the armistice arrived before very much work was done. Following the disbanding of these units, Gosport quickly became surplus to requirements. With a very uncertain future, it became part of No 10 Group, Coastal Area Station and was saved from premanent closure with the reforming of No 186 Squadron on the 13th February 1919. Flying Sopwith Cuckoos, the squadron came to Gosport from HMS Argus and were established as a Torpedo Development Unit.

During the next few years, various types of aircraft were stationed at the base. Blackburn Darts and Bisons, Fairy IIIfs were used mainly in a training role. In December 1936, No 17 Group assumed control of Gosport and at the same time No 813 Squadron FAA formed at the airfield flying the Fairey Swordfish I. Employed in the role of a Torpedo Spotter Reconnaissance Squadron, they eventually embarked on *HMS Eagle*.

As global war once more became a certainty, Gosport began a period of expansion. Unlike most airfields which usually did the reverse, the two tarmac runways were removed in favour of grass. At the same time they were expanded with the SW/NE reaching 2,100 ft and the N/S reaching 1,650 ft. The reason that Gosport had tarmac runways in the beginning was that a solid surface was essential for carrier borne aircraft to practise hard landings for flying and landing on carrier flight decks. With the outbreak of war, most of the aircraft would be embarked on the ships and therefore tarmac landing facilities were not so important.

The autumn of 1938 saw preparations for war going ahead on a large scale. On the 26th September the War Office called out officers and men of anti-aircraft and coast defence units of the Territorial Army. Instructions were also issued by the Home Office to London and many provincial areas for the immediate distribution of gas masks, of which 35 million had already been stored. At Gosport, No 10 Mobilisation Pool was formed and joined the other resident units at the airfield, these being the Group HQ, the Training Squadron, Torpedo Section and No 2 Anti-aircraft Co-operation Unit. The experimental department became the Air Torpedo Development Unit and further building became necessary in the shape of extra hangars as more modern torpedo bombers such as the Bristol Beaufort arrived to be tested.

When war broke it had very little effect on Gosport. Despite the

The Blackburn B6 Shark. (C Samson)

Directive No 1 issued by Adolf Hitler on the 31st August 1939 stating 'In operations against England the task of the Luftwaffe is to take measures to dislocate English imports, the armaments industry, and the transport of troops to France. Any favourable opportunity of an effective attack on concentrated units of the English Navy, particularly on battleships or aircraft carriers, will be exploited. The decision regarding attacks on London is reserved to me'. The first time the enemy flew over Gosport was at 1 pm on Tuesday 5th September, two days after the declaration of war, when a single enemy aircraft approached Portsmouth at 20,000 ft. A yellow warning was issued for the area including the airfield but no bombs were dropped and the enemy climbed away into the cloud. On Tuesday 25th September, the first German aircraft lost in operations against Great Britain was claimed by one of the Blackburn Skuas of a squadron that had flown from Gosport in February and May of 1939. No 803 Squadron of the FAA then operating from *HMS Ark Royal* north of the Great Fisher Bank, was flying several Skuas on a routine patrol. One of the aircraft flown by Lt B S McEwen and Air Gunner Petty Officer Airman B M Seymour shot down a Dornier 18D (0731) of 2/Kustenfliegergruppe 506, one of three on a sortie over the English coast. Landing on the sea, Leutnant zur See Freiherr Von Reitenstein and Lt zur See Korner with two other crew members were rescued before their aircraft was sunk by gunfire from *HMS Somali*.

The rest of September and October saw yellow warnings issued frequently although many of them turned out to be false alarms.

70

Enemy aircraft were sometimes heard in the vicinity but this was the period of the phoney war which lulled everyone into a false sense of security. Gosport continued in the training role although it was obvious to all that the enemy had pinpointed the airfield as a potential target. Though it is often thought that the intention of the Luftwaffe was to only attack Fighter Command airfields, their actual purpose was to knock out any airfield whether fighter, bomber, coastal or training. The Luftwaffe plan for Monday 12th August was to attack the forward fighter airfields of Manston, Lympne and Hawkinge, six radar stations including Ventnor on the Isle of Wight, Portsmouth naval base and a convoy in the Thames Estuary. Also included was Gosport.

From early morning the enemy armadas had crossed the Channel. There had been attacks on two convoys code-named 'Arena and Agent' in the estuary. These had been carried out by JU 87 'Stukas' of the 2nd Gruppe of Stukageschwader 2 and the 3rd Gruppe of Stukageschwader 77. The main target was however Portsmouth, the assault on which was carried out by the JU 88s of KG 51. It was a very heavy attack which seemed to go on unhindered for about 20 minutes. The noise of the exploding bombs could be heard by the navy at Gosport but it was not until around 15 of the JU 88s suddenly dived low over the airfield and dropped a pattern of bombs that the full horror of the onslaught dawned on them. Craters appeared in the grass, dust and smoke rose up to about 100 ft but luckily there was no loss of life nor was any building damaged. As the raid ended, one of the Gosport Skuas flown by P/O 'Nobby' Clarke took off between the craters and headed for Sussex where it was reported a Spitfire had been seen diving into the sea. Crossing the coast at Littlehampton, he found a patch of oil and some wreckage on the sea but no pilot. Turning for home he was chased by a ME 109 but managed to dive down to ground level whereupon the enemy pilot turned and headed for home. Landing carefully back at Gosport, within minutes he had a shovel in his hand and was helping to fill in the craters.

Later that evening the German propaganda machine was in full swing. 'Our glorious Luftwaffe today attacked the great naval base at Portsmouth. Approaching over Spithead, our bombers divided into three groups. One bombed the munitions and mines depot of Priddy's Hard, the second attacked the dockyard and the third the storage tanks and airfield at Gosport. 71 British planes have been destroyed, we have lost 17'. In actual fact Luftflotten 2 and 3 had lost 31 aircraft and the RAF, in the course of 732 sorties, had lost 22. A major blow had however been struck by the Luftwaffe in their attack on Ventnor radar station. Two direct hits broke the masts and fires had been started all over the site, these continuing until late in the evening. Ventnor was out of action for ten days, but luckily this was not known to the enemy. Effective cover from the other radar stations plus a mobile unit ensured that no piece of coastline was unprotected.

The next large raid on Gosport took place on 16th August. Shortly after midday the radar screens showed three heavy formations crossing the Channel. The aircraft approaching Portland, JU 88s from KG 51 and 54, split up and units made for Tangmere, Lee-on-Solent and Gosport. At the latter, 12 bombers escorted by ME 110 fighter/bombers, dived out of the sun just as lunch was being served in the mess. The airfield had received prior warning and many of the personnel were already in the shelters. As the bombs fell, the earth around them seemed to erupt. The noise in the shelters was deafening and the dust and earth falling from the roofs was suffocating. Above, some buildings and a hangar were partly demolished as the one or two Lewis guns used for the defence of Gosport attempted to shoot the enemy down. It was more of a defiant gesture than a serious attempt to immobilise an aircraft that was attacking their home. Being a Coastal Command/FAA airfield, Gosport had thought that a major attack was unlikely and consequently was not fully prepared to deal with such a large attack. Likewise, many of the aircraft mainly Skuas and Rocs were lined neatly up on the hard-standing. As the devastation rained down, nine were set alight and destroyed adding to the smoke and fire already surrounding the entire area. Four people were killed together with two seriously injured and many more with minor injuries.

The enemy however also suffered badly when Fighter Command put up a number of squadrons. One of these was No 249 (Gold Coast) Squadron, flying Hurricanes from Boscombe Down. Scrambled at around 1.15 pm, Red section led by Flt/Lt J B Nicholson were vectored to patrol between Poole and Romsey at 15,000 ft. The aircraft bombing Gosport were soon seen by the section and climbing to 17,000 ft, with the sun behind them, Nicholson led his squadron into a ferocious dogfight. Worried about the sun being behind them, the pilots thoughts were cut short as they were attacked by ME 110s of Zerstorergeschwader 26 and 76. All three aircraft were hit by cannon shells, two of them, including Nicholson's, critically. The third Hurricane flown by Sqd/Ldr E B King managed to make it back to Boscombe Down. Flt/Lt Nicholson, his cockpit a mass of flames, prepared to bale out. Releasing

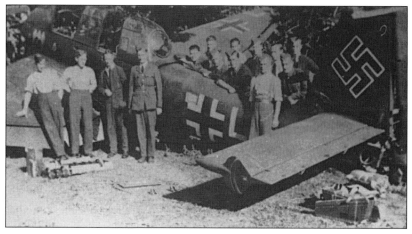

The first Junkers 87 Stuka to fall in Britain was this one, which fell to the guns of No. 145 Squadron and F/O Peter Parrott. It came down at St Lawrence on the Isle of Wight on 8th August 1940. (Plaistow Pictorial)

his harness, he suddenly saw a ME 110 in front of him. Although in a great deal of pain, he carried out an attack on the enemy aircraft. With smoke streaming from it, the ME 110 dived out of sight and Flt/Lt Nicholson prepared to abandon his blazing Hurricane. Very badly burnt he managed to pull the ripcord of his parachute and in agony, drifted down towards the suburbs of Southampton. His ordeal however was not yet over as an over-enthusiastic sergeant in the Home Guard, thinking him a German, fired a shotgun at the descending airman and further injured him with pellets. After admittance to the Royal Southampton Hospital, he was transferred to the RAF hospital at Halton.

Flt/Lt Nicholson eventually recovered from his injuries and on the 15th November 1940 he was awarded the Victoria Cross, the only Battle of Britain pilot to receive this honour.

And so ended the worst day so far for Gosport but the airfield only had one day's relief as the Luftwaffe returned to finish off what they had started. The 18th August has become known as the 'hardest day' throughout the campaign of the Battle of Britain. This was the day that in addition to smaller raids, the Luftwaffe mounted three massive raids against England. This was also the day that the fighter pilots faced their

The Junkers 87 Stuka was the main dive-bomber during the Battle of Britain. This aircraft belongs to 1/StG1. (Bundesarchiv)

greatest challenge. One of these raids was to involve the greatest concentration of JU 87 'Stukas' to be sent across the Channel. The targets were very specific, the airfields at Gosport, Ford and Thorney Island and the radar station at Poling in Sussex. (See *Sussex Airfields in the Second World War.*) The entire force of Stukageschwader 77, whose HQ was at Caen under the command of Major Chemens Graf von Schonborn, was to be committed. In addition, a fighter escort of huge magnitude was to ensure that the Stukas carried out their mission unhindered.

At Gosport, clearance from the previous raids was still going on. With most of the grass runways now patched, attention had been turned to the demolition of what remained standing of the battered buildings and hangars. Given advance warning of the pending attack, all off-duty personnel had taken to the shelters. It was none too soon as Major Eduard Newmann, the commander of the 1st Gruppe of JG 27 who were escorting the Stukas, watched the dive-bombers go into action. Swooping down they dropped their single bomb with precision from around 700 ft. The sounds of huge explosions were heard for

74

miles as each aircraft found its target. Buildings including the engineering workshops were once again wrecked, two more hangars were blown apart wrecking several aircraft that were parked inside and a direct hit on the MT section ensured that many of the vehicles would never move again.

After the noise of exploding bombs, it was suddenly very quiet. As the men and women emerged from the shelters to see what was left of their airfield, the only sound was the crackling of the fires and the sirens of the fire appliances that had raced to the airfield as soon as they saw Gosport being attacked. The ambulances were not needed for despite all the destruction, miraculously there was no loss of life and very little injury.

The Stukas and their fighter escorts suffered grievously at the hands of Fighter Command as many squadrons caught the Luftwaffe turning for home. The Tangmere squadrons, Nos 43 and 601 with Hurricanes together with No 602 flying Spitfires from the satellite airfield of Westhampnett, hurled themselves into the fray. Though some aircraft and pilots were lost, it was nothing compared to the German losses.

As the day drew to a close, Fighter Command had flown 766 sorties and together with the ack-ack guns had shot down 71 enemy aircraft. In contrast, 27 RAF fighters had been lost with ten pilots killed. The day was significant however, for this was the last time that the Stuka was used over mainland Britain. The recent losses had been so great that the German High Command realised that its effective day was over and it was therefore pulled out of the front line.

The repair of Gosport took a considerable time and long afterwards there were tales of the personnel's heroism. New buildings and hangars had to be constructed and a lot of repair work went into the underground shelters to make them safer. It was not until the 6th December 1940 that the airfield was in a fit state to accept a resident squadron. Reforming at Gosport, No 86 Squadron received their Blenheim IVs and immediately began working up to operational status in order to begin convoy escort duties along the east coast. They departed for Leuchars shortly after Christmas 1940 leaving the Air Training Development Unit at Gosport alone once again.

By June 1941 the night blitz by the Luftwaffe was over but for Coastal Command there was no respite. Experiments on different ways to drop torpedos from aircraft were continuing at Gosport and for this task a variety of aircraft were used. Hampdens, Wellingtons, Beauforts and Manchesters, all of them were necessary in the job to perfect a sure way of dropping torpedos or mines. In May 1941, the first Beaufighter arrived for drop trials and this saw the start of a very hectic period.

The FAA maintenance unit that had been stationed at Gosport for some time became No 3502 Servicing Unit as the airfield was transferred back to No 16 Group Coastal Command, whose HQ had recently moved from Lee-on-Solent to Chatham in Kent. Hudsons arrived for the first time on the 27th August 1942 when No 608 (North Riding) Auxiliary Squadron arrived to be fitted with long range fuel tanks. They were followed by the same type belonging to No 500 (County of Kent) Auxiliary Squadron and when they had been fitted with long range tanks, both squadrons left for North Africa in connection with 'Operation Torch', the invasion of French North Africa which took place in October 1942.

From this time various squadrons rotated through Gosport in connection with the ATDU. One that remained until the 20th December 1945 was No 667 Squadron. Formed at Gosport on the 1st December 1943 from the remains of Nos 1662 and 1631 Flights, it was equipped with the Boulton Paul Defiant employed in target towing duties. There followed a variety of aircraft including Barracudas, Vengeances, Hurricanes and Oxfords, all of them becoming very familiar sights around Hampshire. Work was still taking place repairing much of the damage caused by the raids of 1940 as further lodger units used the Gosport facilities. The run-up to D Day had very little effect on the airfield, training continuing as usual. In January 1945 the airfield was returned fully to the navy and it became HMS Siskin. Victory was celebrated in the form of a fly-past of the aircraft present at that time followed by festivities on the base.

HMS Siskin saw many naval squadrons pass through during 1945/ 46 including Nos 764, 667, 778 and 727 Squadrons. It continued in the training role but with defence spending becoming an issue as early as 1956, Gosport became surplus to requirements. The last unit to leave the airfield, the ATDU, left for Culdrose in 1956 after 38 years at the base. HMS Siskin was paid off in June 1956 and Gosport became just another empty wartime airfield.

On the 28th May 1957, a plaque was unveiled at the site to commemorate all who had served there. The expansion of a nearby naval housing estate began to encroach upon the airfield and soon very little of the grass used by the aircraft of Coastal Command and the FAA remained. Gosport was an important training airfield and was certainly an invaluable part of the fight to defeat the enemy.

10

LASHAM

Lasham had no First World War history nor had it been built by the time the Battle of Britain began. Situated five miles south-east of Basingstoke, authorisation only came in September 1941 for land to be requisitioned for a satellite airfield for the bomber airfield at Aldermaston. Construction was given to McAlpines who built a standard hard three runway site with dispersal areas and hard-standings, hangars, technical areas and accommodation blocks. In the meantime, plans for Aldermaston had been changed and in place of the expected OTU for bombers, it was handed over to the USAAF. This had a knock-on effect for Lasham as in the autumn of 1942, No 38 Wing of Army Co-operation Command gained control of the airfield.

The change however did nothing to bring Lasham into operation and it says little for the enemy's intelligence service when the airfield was bombed in 1942, months before it was even completed! Its first introduction to operational status came on the 11th March 1943 when No 175 Squadron, whose motto was aptly 'Stop at Nothing', arrived with Hurricane IIBs. It was during 1943 that large scale exercises for the Army and RAF were held. Code-named 'Spartan', they were part of the preparations for D-Day and involved many squadrons flying tank-busting Hurricanes. No 175 Squadron were part of No 124 Airfield, 2 Group and although they stayed for just a brief period at Lasham, they were later followed by No 412 (Falcon) Squadron of the RCAF flying Spitfire VBs, No 181 Squadron with Typhoon IBs, No 602 (City of Glasgow) Auxiliary Squadron with Spitfire VBs and finally, Nos 182 and 183 (Gold Coast) Squadrons who eventually formed a Typhoon wing. Silence however returned to Lasham when No 124 Airfield

Lasham photographed from 2000 ft by the RAF in October 1942. Not yet operational, it shows signs of main runway construction. (RAF Museum)

moved to the ALG at Apuldram in Sussex on 2nd June 1943. No 10 Group Fighter Command assumed command of Lasham before No 2 Group of the Tactical Air Force took over on 28th August 1943.

One of the allied squadrons to fly with Fighter Command was No 320 (Netherlands) Squadron. When the Germans invaded Holland several Fokker T-VIIIW seaplanes were flown to Britain to escape German hands. Arriving at Pembroke Dock they formed No 320 Squadron on 1st June 1940. Transferring to No 2 Group in March 1943, they converted to the American Mitchell II which they brought to Lasham on the 30th August 1943. As part of the 2nd TAF and flying from Lasham, they began attacking enemy communication targets and airfields.

In September 1943, an operation was conceived to confuse the enemy into believing that a landing by the allies was imminent along the beaches of the Pas-de-Calais. Code-named 'Starkey', it entailed massive bombing raids along this stretch of the French coast.

Joining 320 Squadron came No 613 (City of Manchester) Auxiliary Squadron flying the North American Mustang I. Unlike other American fighters supplied to the RAF, the Mustang I was built to

RAF requirements and not a doctored version of an American fighter. Making its maiden flight on 1st May 1941, the first production aircraft reached Britain in November 1941. No 613 Squadron used the type on escort and ground attack missions in addition to a tactical reconnaissance role. Although the Mustang proved successful in both roles, the squadron converted to the Mosquito VI shortly after arrival at Lasham, and No 305 (Weilkopolski) Polish Squadron did the same upon their leaving Swanton Morley for Lasham on the 18th November.

From November onwards the squadrons concentrated on low and high level attacks on enemy transport and airfields. Not a day passed without one or all of the squadrons roaming over enemy territory looking for suitable targets. They encountered some resistance from ground fire and enemy aircraft but with the war now going the way of the allies, the aircraft were able to do a lot of damage to the enemy.

With the addition of No 107 Squadron who flew in from Hartford-bridge (Blackbushe) in February 1944, No 138 Airfield became an entire Mosquito wing. Attacks were carried out on the strange ramp-like structures that had been seen along the French coast. These missions were known as 'Noball' and the ramps that had been photographed were in fact the launch pads for Hitler's revenge weapon, the V1 or 'Doodlebug'. Having been advised by a scientist, Dr R V Jones, for some time Duncan Sandys, the son-in-law of Winston Churchill, had been sure that the Germans were carrying out rocket trials. Photographs taken by reconnaissance aircraft plus the information from agents in France, later indicated that his worst fears had been realised. Immediately the US 8th Air Force began bombing the No ball sites by day eventually dropping over 23,000 tons of bombs between February and June 1944. The RAF also did enormous damage to the rocket sites; but for these attacks, Hitler's rocket campaign may well have lasted much longer.

As D-Day approached, No 138 Airfield was tasked with the job of attacking communication targets in France. Some operations were more spectacular than others but all of them contributed greatly to the overall impact of D-Day. Precision attacks were also the job of No 138 Wing who together with No 140 Wing, caused great consternation to the enemy in retreat.

One particular raid worthy of mention was carried out on 30th June 1944. It had been known for some time that a large chateau at Chateuneve du France near Brest was used as a rest centre for German submarine crews. U-boat crews were becoming very scarce at this period of the war and it was felt that if an attack could be carried out whilst the chateau was full, the service would be even thinner on crews. The CO of No 138 Wing, G/Capt L W Bowser, calculated that six Mosquitos would be needed to complete the task. Leaving Lasham on 23rd June before light, the wing approached the French coast only to find it covered in fog. Despite several attempts to get under or around the fog, it was to no avail and the mission had to be aborted.

The following Sunday, 30th June, the weather forecast was optimistic as the six aircraft once again climbed away from Lasham. Although the Channel was clear, cloud over the French coast was down to about 200 ft. Skilfully leading the wing, G/Capt Bowser flew along the valleys below cloud until the chateau came into sight. Coming in low over the ornamental gardens, all the aircraft dropped their bombs with pin-point accuracy. News from the French Resistance later confirmed that the raid had been an outstanding success and that the chateau at the time had about 400 German sailors as guests. Another example of accuracy was the occasion on which six Mosquitos of 138 Wing attacked a building in Holland which was being used by the Germans to store Gestapo records. Attacking from 50 ft, not a single bomb missed its mark. Some were seen actually going through the front door! All that remained of the building after the attack was a smouldering heap with every single record destroyed.

It was not until October 1944 that No 138 Airfield moved on to Hartfordbridge (Blackbushe). For several weeks after this hectic period Lasham was deserted but the 27th November saw No 84 Group Support Unit arrive from Thruxton. The airfield became designated a satellite to Blackbushe and came within the fold of No 11 Group, Fighter Command. Now that the war was coming to an end, the task of the support unit was to dispose of certain types of aircraft. Lasham became more of a maintenance airfield than an operational one during this period and when the European war ended in May 1945, the end to military operations came quickly. Lasham was closed on 26th October 1948 but not before permission had been given to use the airfield for gliding. Transferred to the Ministry of Aviation on 15th July 1961, Dan Air Engineering set up their main base at the airfield. The airline flew for many years until the crippling recession of 1991 brought about its demise. Luckily the gliders remained and kept the airfield open and since that time, the 1,797 yard asphalt runway has attracted a lot of business and executive jet aircraft.

11
LEE-ON-SOLENT

There is no doubt that one of the more remarkable FAA aircraft of the
Second World War was the Fairey Swordfish. Known affectionately as
the 'Stringbag', it saw squadron service from 1936 until the very last
one was retired from active service in 1953. Today only two airworthy
examples remain, both of them flying with the Royal Naval Historical
Flight at Yeovilton. It is also the one aircraft that is associated with
most naval airfields including Lee-on-Solent where most of the
squadrons that were based there during the war flew the Swordfish
at one time or another. This long association with the aircraft is
commemorated by a public house named The Swordfish which is
situated very close to the airfield at Lee.

With the increase in enemy submarine activity around the British
mainland and the loss of many convoys, it was felt by the authorities in
the spring of 1917 that more seaplane bases were needed to combat the
U-boat menace. Selecting a site on the western edge of Lee-on-Solent
town where it runs down to a gravel beach and then to the sea, the
Naval Seaplane Training School opened on 30th July 1917. By 1st April
1918 it was transferred to the Air Ministry and became part of No 10
Group RAF. It continued in a training role until reduced to Care and
Maintenance in December 1919. Re-opened on 1st June 1920, once
again as a seaplane training base, it was renamed the School of Naval
Co-operation in 1923. A variety of aircraft including Fairey IIIDs and
Ospreys were soon passing through Lee which continued in a similar
vein until 1938 when, with the war clouds looming over Europe, the
pace quickened. The School of Naval Co-operation moved out and a
Station headquarters was established to administer the Home Fleet

The faithful Walrus air/sea rescue aircraft. The saviour of many airmen. (MAP)

Catapult Flights and a number of FAA squadrons. As with the rapid expansion of the RAF, the FAA did likewise and on the 24th May 1939, Lee was taken over fully by the Admiralty and became HMS Daedalus. In this new role the airfield was expanded with building taking the priority. As war approached the Seaplane Training School became No 765 Squadron but it continued in the role of training seaplane pilots and as a reserve for catapult squadrons. This time, in addition to the Swordfish, the faithful Supermarine Walrus, known to all aircrew as the 'Shagbat' was used. Its reputation was only rivalled by the aforementioned Swordfish. Although single engined, its reliability and durability became legend. Known as the eyes of the fleet it was also used in the ASR role to great effect. Its usefulness to the FAA can be gauged by the fact that Supermarine built 287 amphibians followed later by 453 built by Saunders Roe before production ceased in January 1944.

The 23rd August 1939 saw No 710 Squadron form at Lee equipped once again with the Walrus. It was designated a Seaplane Squadron for service aboard *HMS Albatross*. After training at Lee and a move to Mount Batten, 710 embarked on the carrier on 1st September 1939 and the ship sailed for West Africa.

Preparations for all-out war continued at Lee. Shelters were dug,

82

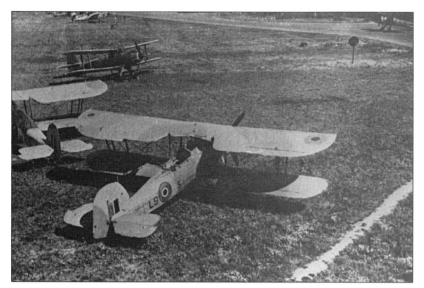

The venerable Fairey Swordfish of No 781 Squadron based at Lee-on-Solent in 1939. (FAA Museum)

camouflage was hastily applied to all the buildings and gun posts were placed at strategic points around the airfield. Though still a training airfield, no effort was spared in denying the enemy an obvious target. On the morning of Sunday 3rd September 1939, all the naval personnel gathered around their wireless sets to hear Mr Chamberlain speak. When he had finished there was silence. No one at that time knew that around the same time, the *SS Athenia* had been torpedoed by a U-boat and had sunk 250 miles off the Donegal coast. Whilst the majority of the crew were saved unbeknown to the personnel at Lee, the opening shots of the war had already been fired.

Shortly after the outbreak of war, No 778 Squadron formed at Lee. Equipped with Swordfish, Walrus, Skuas and Rocs, it was a Service Trials Unit commanded by L/Cdr R A Kilroy RN. They were joined by No 770 Squadron on 7th November equipped with Skuas, Rocs, Sea Gladiators and Swordfish. Designated a Deck Landing Training Squadron, they stayed for two days before embarking on *HMS Argus* for the Mediterranean. Such was the rapid movements of the FAA squadrons at this period.

Christmas 1939 was spent quietly at Lee-on-Solent. As there was no immediate threat of war, most of the naval personnel in training were given leave. With the new year things began to change and the Dunkirk evacuation brought a new feel to the war at Lee.

As the remaining army of the BEF withdrew to the port of Dunkirk, the RAF and the FAA briefed their pilots to keep the skies above them clear of German aircraft. An armada of craft crossed the Channel to rescue the men from the beaches; the troops remained scattered about the sand dunes until the moment came for embarkation, then went down to the beach in batches and clambered onto whatever craft had come ashore for them.

As the days wore on, the stream of soldiers increased and more and more aircraft were given the task of protecting them. Some of the aircraft used by the FAA were totally unsuitable for the task. Skuas and Rocs, mainly used for target towing, were thrown into the role of fighters. At Lee-on-Solent, both types together with the Swordfish, were prepared for action over Dunkirk. It was hoped that their presence alone would deter the Luftwaffe from attacking the beaches. For L/Cdr P G Bryant RN, the CO of No 778 Squadron, the idea of using these aircraft in a fighter role was frightening. The Blackburn Skua was a two-seat deck-landing fighter and dive-bomber and the Blackburn Roc was a two-seat fleet fighter with a power driven turret placed behind the pilot. Neither aircraft had any forward firing guns at all. With very little protection for the crews and no comparitive fire-power to the RAF fighters, Lt/Cdr Bryant felt it was certain suicide to send his crews in. For the beleaguered army at Dunkirk, it did not matter what aircraft were in the sky as long as it kept 'Jerry' from above their heads.

Some of these aircraft did not get back to Lee and the ones that did usually came in with battle damage everywhere. The ground-crews worked tirelessly to get the aircraft repaired and back into the air for the next day. Like the rest of the stations Lee-on-Solent was working flat out for 24 hours, 7 days a week. When it was all over, Mr Churchill announced to the world that 'our airforce decisively defeated the main strength of the German Air Force'. This of course included the FAA squadrons. A tribute by the enemy was added to Mr Churchill's words when Berlin Radio announced, 'We must admit, the British fighters were magnificent'. Whilst there was no victory at Dunkirk, there was a victory in the miracle of the deliverance of the BEF from France.

With the crisis over, Lee-on-Solent returned to its training role. On 8th April 1940, No 704 Squadron had formed at the airfield with L/Cdr

F E C Judd RN as CO. Equipped with Walrus, Swordfish and Seafox aircraft, they moved to Pembroke Dock before Lee came to the attention of the Luftwaffe. For some time German reconnaissance aircraft had been flying over and around the airfield whilst carrying out photographic sorties over the Portland area. One particular aircraft came closer than normal on the 8th and it became clear to all that the airfield was soon to receive a visit from the Luftwaffe.

It was in fact on Friday 16th August that two major attacks took place, one of them causing serious damage to Lee. The day dawned sunny and warm and with a little high cloud. The radar plots remained quiet until just after 11 am when a series of raids was levelled against Norfolk and Kent. Just after midday more raiders were seen approaching with the first 50 aircraft making for the Thames Estuary, the next 150 for Dover and the remaining 100 going for the Portsmouth and Southampton area. Despite being intercepted by the RAF fighters, the majority of the bombers got through with 12 of them heading for Lee-on-Solent.

It was the JU 87s of Stukageschwader 2 operating from Lannion that had the airfield squarely in their sights. A short distance away the same was happening at Gosport. As the Stukas commenced their dive, everyone not on essential duty dived for the newly-dug shelters. Above, the aircraft released their bombs at around 700 ft and continuing to howl, pulled up steeply from their dive. With a tremendous explosion the bombs hit the earth followed by smoke and flame rising high into the afternoon sky. The other sound was that of the airfield gunners blazing away at the enemy with their hopelessly inadequate Lewis guns. It was a defiant gesture but that was all. The Stukas had it all their own way. There were direct hits on the two main hangars destroying all the aircraft that were inside. Most of the aircraft parked outside were no longer to be seen, there just remained pieces of air-frame burning furiously. Thick smoke covered the entire area, choking anyone who had dared to venture out of the shelters. Despite the intense devastation, there was no loss of life. Slowly the off-duty personnel emerged from safety, many of the Wrens in tears for this was their first baptism of war. Looking around, it was difficult to remember how everything had looked a few minutes before the Stukas began their reign of terror. As the fire engines and ambulances converged on Lee, the enemy was heading for home. They were caught by the Hurricanes of No 1 Squadron from Northolt and the Hurricanes of No 43 Squadron from Tangmere and immediately a fierce battle began between the escorting German fighters and the two squadrons. Both sides lost aircraft but at the end of the day it was the Luftwaffe that suffered most. In the 24 hours of the 16th, they had flown 1,715 sorties for the loss of 45 aircraft and many good aircrew. The RAF had 22 fighters shot down with eight pilots killed. There were of course a large number of aircraft destroyed on the ground but these were not fighters. Again, eight airfields were hit but only three of them were part of Fighter Command. Once more German intelligence had got it completely wrong.

Slowly, life got back to something approaching normality. For several days after the attack, the sirens could be heard wailing over Portsmouth and Southampton but there were no further attacks upon Lee. It is appropriate at this stage to list the air-raid warning system in use during this period of the battle. The colour code was as follows:

1. Yellow, issued by Fighter Command as a preliminary to all areas over which raiders might pass.

2. Purple, issued at night to areas in the course of raiders. On receipt of this, all exposed lighting in docks, factories etc had to be extinguished.

3. Red, a public warning upon receipt of which the sirens sounded.

In addition to these standard warnings, the local Observer Corps always contacted Lee-on-Solent when they plotted raiders approaching.

The month of September 1940 was designated the fourth phase of the battle. In the Germans' opinion, the attacks on airfields around the south-east and on London itself had cleared the way for the final assault before invasion could take place. Although enemy aircraft were often in the vicinity of Lee, the only other time that it was attacked was on the 11th September when during a raid on Southampton, some of the bombers of Luftflotte 3 dropped several bombs around the perimeter. Very little damage was caused apart from a few large holes in the runway which were soon patched up.

The main target of the Luftwaffe during October was London and again, the German losses proved very high with 325 aircraft lost. Since July 10th a total of 1,733 enemy aircraft had been destroyed with the RAF losing 915. By November it was over and the air war was about to enter a new phase.

On 27th December 1940, No 702 Squadron reformed at Lee as a long range catapult squadron with Fairey Seafoxes for duty in armed merchant cruisers. By the new year much of the repair work at Lee was

A Firebrand TF11 of No 708 Squadron, Lee-on-Solent. (MAP)

still to be done and the task of rebuilding the airfield was to continue until late 1941.

With the fall of France in 1940, a number of aircraft fell into German hands. One particular type was the Vought V-156 which had been ordered from the Americans by the French for their Naval Air Service. Deliveries had just begun when the Germans invaded France and took them over. It is rumoured that a few of them were used by the Luftwaffe in the Battle of Britain though this is not confirmed. With the capture of France, Britain took the remaining contract on board and received a number of aircraft, calling them Chesapeake Is. The first operational squadron to receive them was No 811 which reformed at Lee-on-Solent on 15th July 1941 as a Torpedo Bomber Reconnaissance Squadron. They received 14 of the type plus two Sea Hurricanes. The aircraft soon proved unsuitable for escort carrier work and was eventually relegated to training duties. No 811 Squadron used the Chesapeake until November 1941 when they gladly converted to the Swordfish.

Lee continued in the training role for the rest of the year with very little change. As aircraft became larger and more powerful, it was decided to extend the airfield and in 1942, a 3,000 ft tarmac runway was laid with a secondary strip of 2,400 ft. Additional dispersal areas were built and Lee-on-Solent prepared for an increase in usage.

On 12th January 1942 a decision made in Germany by Hitler and his commanders-in-chief was to have a far reaching impact on life at Lee. It had been known to the Air Ministry and the Admiralty as early as April 1941 that at least two German capital ships would leave Brest on the French coast and travel to a German port via the English Channel. When this happened it would give the RAF and the Navy the best opportunity ever to engage the enemy ships whilst in the Straits of Dover. Accordingly, plans were made well in advance to intercept and destroy the *Scharnhorst* and *Gneisnau* while they were at their closest point to the shores of Britain. In the event, the plans turned into a fiasco and caused Britain to sustain one of its most humiliating defeats of the war.

The operation was initially code-named 'Fuller', this code being used purely for the time of the break-out from Brest Harbour. For some time submarines and reconnaissance aircraft had been keeping an eye on the German ships for any signs of possible movement and it was on receipt of 'Fuller' that all forces could be mobilised.

At Lee, No 825 Squadron had reformed on 1st January 1942 with six Swordfish Is for Torpedo Bomber reconnaissance duties. Commanded by L/Cdr Eugene Esmonde DSO, RN they were fresh from a recent successful operation in helping to sink another capital German ship, the *Bismark*. Together with six Swordfish aircraft came seven pilots, six observers and six air gunners, of whom only two of the pilots and four of the observers had any operational experience. Esmonde had been a pilot with Imperial Airways before the war and had joined the FAA at the outbreak. His squadron, 815, had been aboard *HMS Ark Royal* when she was sunk on 13th November 1941. Whilst all its Swordfish aircraft were lost, the crews survived and it was these gallant men that, together with their CO, reformed No 825 Squadron at Lee.

During January, the airfield echoed to the sound of Bristol Pegasus engines as Esmonde began to bring his crews up to operational standards. Night and day it was a programme of mock torpedo attacks, practising taking evasive action from enemy aircraft and low level mock attacks on naval shipping in the Solent. With a top speed of only 90 knots, the squadron knew that if called upon to attack the enemy fleet without fighter cover in daylight, they would be in the greatest danger of being shot out of the sky. Thus the better they rehearsed the tactics the more chance they would have of staying alive. Esmonde himself hoped that more Swordfish would be allocated to his squadron at Lee-on-Solent to give them a better striking chance, but none were forthcoming.

The weather was not very conducive to flying at this time with snow and low cloud proving a problem. During the last week in January the crews were briefed on the type of attack to be carried out should the enemy fleet break cover. Intelligence had passed the news that a third ship was included in the armada, the heavy cruiser *Prinz Eugen*, making the task even more hazardous. Senior RAF and Naval personnel attended the briefing in an atmosphere that was very charged. The squadron retired that evening tired and brooding on the possible outcome of the action. The mess at Lee that evening was strangely empty and quiet.

The evening of the last day of January saw everyone wondering just when the break out would occur. Just after midnight, L/Cdr Esmonde was awakened and told it appeared that the ships were getting ready to move out of Brest. The squadron came to 15 minutes readiness and were given attack orders. By dawn it became apparent it was a false alarm and the exhausted men were stood down. Back at the Air Ministry, it was decided that Lee was too far away to get the aircraft quickly into a striking position and 825 were sent down to the forward airfield at Manston, the closest base to the Straits of Dover. A few days later the Swordfish departed and headed for Manston leaving Lee to await the results of the impending action.

History records the failed attempts to destroy the German fleet when it finally sailed into the Straits. For the six Swordfish of 825 it was a bitter tragedy as Esmonde led his gallant men into the attack. With no real fighter protection due to a variety of misjudgements, all of the aircraft were shot down with no torpedo hits being registered on any of the enemy. Sadly many of the Swordfish crews perished in the attack including the CO himself. For his bravery he was awarded a posthumous VC, and the five surviving crew members were all decorated. The enemy ships sailed through the Straits unhindered and only at the last minute did the *Scharnhorst* strike a mine. It caused the ship very little trouble and the Germans reached a home port safely.

Sometime later a board of inquiry was convened to find out just what went wrong and how the enemy had managed to sail through the

A Barracuda II airborne from Lee-on-Solent. No 798 Squadron flew this type from October 1943 to June 1945. (Crown copyright)

Straits directly under the nose of the British. The incident became known as the 'war's greatest blunder' and added insult to the great loss of so many FAA pilots.

'Like a Thunderbolt from Heaven' was the motto of No 810 Squadron who re-equipped at Lee in April 1943 with the Fairey Barracuda. Intended as a replacement for the Albacore, 810 became the second unit to fly the type. An aggressive aircraft in appearance, it was used in the torpedo bomber reconnaissance role and certainly became a 'thunderbolt from heaven' with its powerful Rolls Royce Merlin engine. Staying little more than a month, 810 moved to Machrihanish on the 21st May 1943.

Over the next six months, various other Barracuda equipped squadrons arrived and departed from Lee. Many of them flew in for a period of conversion flying before embarking on carriers. This theme continued until 1944 when, with D-Day rapidly approaching, the FAA took on more responsibility for keeping the sky clear of enemy aircraft above the landing troops. Many squadrons now became part of the 2nd TAF whilst others formed special naval fighter wings. February 1944 saw Nos 808, 886 and 897 Squadrons form No 3 Naval Fighter Wing mainly flying the Supermarine Seafire, a naval version of the Spitfire.

They were mainly employed on spotting and reconnaissance duties connected with D-Day. In preparation, invasion stripes were painted on the wings of all aircraft flying in support of the landings to enable better identification. The 21st May 1944 saw No 897 Squadron bring their new Spitfire LVbs to Lee. Commanded by L/Cdr W C Simpson, they joined the other squadrons in providing top cover for the invading allies. From dawn, all the squadrons were on standby. Many were airborne by early morning but it was No 897 Squadron who got first blood when they shot down a ME 109 and attacked a German midget submarine. All the following day the pace continued to involve every unit. Several RAF squadrons joined the FAA in using Lee-on-Solent as their base and at the end of a very hectic period involving 453 sorties, Lee could lay claim to flying the largest number of all the TAF bases.

With the allies firmly established in France, the call upon the airfield diminished and the fighter wing disbanded on 15th July. The squadrons dispersed to other bases and Lee was left to the Barracudas and No 781 Squadron who had been resident since 1940 although aircraft were dispersed to other airfields.

In November 1944, No 1700 Squadron formed as an Amphibian Bomber Reconnaissance Squadron and flew the Supermarine Sea Otter, the successor to the faithful Walrus. They took delivery of six aircraft which were used not only for reconnaissance duties but also in the ASR role. The type eventually outlived its predecessor by six years and was the last large biplane in FAA service. A further six aircraft were allocated to No 1701 Squadron which also formed at Lee in February 1945 before embarking on *HMS Begun* in April.

So Lee-on-Solent approached the end of its war. It had certainly had its fair share of enemy attacks yet it remained, like its near neighbour Gosport, basically a training airfield. It provided many famous squadrons that had eventually embarked onto carriers and carried the war to distant lands. Now as peace approached, its role as a training establishment was set to continue.

The post-war period again saw many famous squadrons use the facilities at Lee. It became the FAA's major technical training establishment and was renamed HMS Ariel in October 1959 at the same time as the Air Electrical School moved in from Worthy Down. In 1962 the inter-service hovercraft trials were carried out at Lee and three years later, HMS Ariel became HMS Daedalus. The role of the station, in addition to training, increased to include aircraft employed on fishery protection work, search and rescue and VIP communications.

Lee-on-Solent in 1991, showing the superb standard Royal Navy pattern control tower. (Portsmouth Publishing)

These duties continued throughout the 70s but with the economic squeeze of the 80s, many of them disappeared and HMS Daedalus prepared for the worst.

Despite all the rumours and fears, the airfield survived and is still today a naval aerodrome. It is used by a mixture of military and civilian aircraft and is also the headquarters of the Naval Gliding Club. With the Royal Naval Air Yard of Fleetlands just a few miles away, helicopters such as Lynx and Sea King make use of the airfield at all times. Its one remaining runway, 05/23 is now 1,309 metres long and is capable of handling most modern aircraft types. The Swordfish public house is a veritable treasure trove of nostalgia and is a constant and permanent reminder of Lee-on-Solent during the Second World War.

12
MIDDLE WALLOP

In 1940, night-fighting was very much in its infancy. In a stop-gap measure to counter the enemy aircraft that flew at random most nights over the country, Bristol Blenheim bombers were hastily converted to fighters by adding four machine guns contained in a gun-pack beneath the fuselage in addition to the forward firing turret. Known as the Blenheim IF night-fighter, over 200 were converted by the RAF from kits supplied by the Southern Railway's Ashford factory. Although the aircraft had proved inadequate as a day-fighter, by June 1940 they had been fitted with 'magic mirrors', as some aircrew called them, which were really the first of the airborne interception radar kits for 'seeing in the dark'. The equipment consisted of a radio transmitter and receiver and the necessary aerials which were attached to the Blenheim. An electrical impulse was sent out from one of the aerials which covered an arc of airspace in front of the aircraft. If the signal hit an enemy aircraft it was reflected back to the Blenheim and displayed on a cathode ray tube inside the cockpit and from this 'blip', the range and speed of the enemy aircraft could be deduced.

No 604 (County of Middlesex) Squadron of the Royal Auxiliary Air Force had re-equipped with the Blenheim IF in January 1939 whilst stationed at North Weald. The 3rd July saw them at Gravesend and on the 26th, the squadron moved to a large and unfinished grass airfield in Hampshire. Within easy bombing range of the Luftwaffe, they felt that at last contact would be made with the enemy at night. The airfield they were to operate from had the oddly sounding name of Middle Wallop.

Plans for the new aerodrome, situated five miles west of Andover,

A Bristol Blenheim I, the mainstay of the early fighter and night-fighter squadrons that flew from Middle Wallop. This aircraft belongs to 90 Squadron. (MAP)

began to take shape in 1935. A compulsory purchase was made of Ringwould Farm and another known only as Hungary Hunt. It was planned that Middle Wallop would be an operational station in the newly established Bomber Command and accordingly the messes and barrack blocks were built to accommodate a very large number of air-crews and ground-crews. Likewise, five large 'C' type hangars were constructed to house the bombers and a bomb dump was established in a remote corner of the new station.

Building was carried out by Messrs Higgs and Hill plus several sub-contractors after the initial clearance of the ground by Messrs Raynor Brothers. Despite heavy rain during November 1938, progress was apparent. By the time the Battle of Britain began, most buildings had been started, one of the hangars had the roof on and the landing ground was being prepared and seeded. Delays were caused by the bitter winter of 1939/40 as snow continued to fall together with very hard frosts at night. Despite this however, the SHQ was ready for the keys to be handed over to the RAF on 16th April 1940.

In between times the designation of Middle Wallop had changed and though intended to be a bomber station, it became operational on 12th July 1940 as a training airfield. Despite the construction still continuing,

*RAF Middle Wallop pictured on 1st May 1940. One of the first expansion airfields.
(Public Record Office)*

No 15 Flying Training School arrived from Lossiemouth in Scotland. They found a station in chaos! Mud, wet chalk and builders rubble lay everywhere. With the accommodation still not finished, the airmen were billeted in tents or in the newly constructed married quarters whilst the officers had to endure a journey to RAF Andover.

Although the buildings were not finished, the landing area proved adequate for the twin-engined Airspeed Oxford and Miles Master trainer. The grass measured 1,000 yard SE-NW, 1,250 yards E-W, 1,200 yards N-S and 1,400 yards NE-SW and a 50 ft concrete perimeter track ran around the airfield. Amidst all this chaos, G/Cpt P E Maitland arrived to take over the position of station commander. It was not an enviable task. Cooking was done in field kitchens, the latrines were not yet ready and there was a shortage of drinkable water, all of which did not please the poor airmen.

The Sector Operations room at Middle Wallop showing the controllers on the left-hand side and the WAAF plotters in the middle. The layout is similar to all the Sector Stations. (Hampshire Record Office)

Despite everything, No 15 FTS were soon airborne and carrying out pilot training. It was part of this training programme that caused the first fatal accident at Middle Wallop when acting P/O Croom-Johnson flying a Master and performing solo aerobatics, crashed to his death alongside the Portsmouth road. Climbing vertically into cloud at around 3,000 ft, the aircraft emerged and went into a spin. Both elevators appeared to break away as the aircraft plunged into soft ground and caught fire. The tragedy shook both military and civilian personnel alike.

Meanwhile, construction continued and those buildings that were ready for occupation were hastily camouflaged. With the Battle of Britain about to break in the skies above, it was decided by the Air Ministry that Middle Wallop was an ideal base for fighter aircraft. A new fighter group was hurriedly formed taking the number 10 with its headquarters at Rudloe Manor in Wiltshire under the command of Air Vice Marshal Sir Quintin Brand. As with the other fighter groups,

A souvenir postcard of the period drawn by Doug Littlejohn. (Border Arts)

certain airfields within the group became sector or controlling stations and Middle Wallop the sector station of sector 'Y'. This incurred the additional building of an operations room, for without this Middle Wallop could not direct its own squadrons within the framework of the group operations room at Rudloe Manor.

The scene was therefore set for Middle Wallop to play a vital role in the defeat of the enemy. With its new status, No 15 FTS moved out on the 11th June 1940, part of it moving to South Cerney and part to Kidlington. Before this, Middle Wallop saw the arrival of one of the squadrons that had witnessed the Dunkirk evacuation. No 601 (County of London) Squadron of the Royal Auxiliary Air Force had been based at Merville in France giving top cover to the beleaguered troops at Dunkirk. As the BEF sailed for Britain and the Germans closed in on the Channel ports, 601 left on the 22nd May and their battle-scarred Hurricanes flew into Middle Wallop on 1st June 1940.

The airfield opened for operations on 12th June 1940 despite building

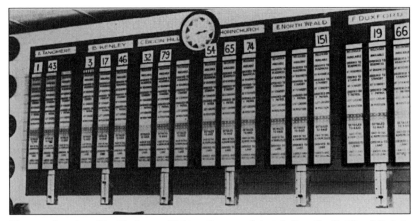

The tote board at No 11 Group Fighter Command just before the Battle of Britain began. (Crown copyright)

continuing. Some airfield defences were now in place including a huge searchlight. Small arms were issued to all the personnel in case of a parachutist attack. There had already been one false alarm when at midnight on the 7th June, flares were dropped on the aerodrome. Immediately the station went to a 'red alert' as further messages were received that parachutists were landing nearby. The army defence team under their commander, Brigadier Lewis, drove around the airfield, guns at the ready. The scare continued and at 1.20 am the Andover police telephoned a series of warnings stating the enemy troops had landed. Too late to quash the rumours and fears, Boscombe Down rang the station to say that experiments were being carried out in the area with aircraft towing flares to light up enemy aircraft. It was this that had set off alarm bells!

As Middle Wallop was stood down, Rudloe Manor, HQ of No 10 Group, became operational and at midday on the 4th August 1940, Middle Wallop and sector 'Y' became active. By this time there were three squadrons on strength. No 238 who brought their Spitfire Is from Tangmere on the 20th June, No 609 (West Riding) Squadron of the Royal Auxiliary Air Force arrived from Northolt on the 5th July 1940 also with Spitfire Is and the aforementioned No 604 (County of Middlesex) Auxiliary Squadron who brought their Blenheims in from Gravesend. Although the station was not yet fully functional, Middle Wallop prepared to go to war.

Hawker Hurricane Mk IIs of No 601 (County of London) Squadron Royal Auxiliary Air Force airborne from Middle Wallop in 1940. (IWM)

With the battle now raging overhead, some of the aircraft from 609 flew to the forward and satellite airfield of Warmwell. Arriving as dawn broke, they stayed until sunset before returning to Middle Wallop. No 238 Squadron exchanged their Spitfires for Hurricane Is and 604 were busy developing night-fighting techniques. With all this activity, it was not long before the Luftwaffe paid the airfield a visit.

The usual pattern for the station at this time was to fly daily patrols, some from Wallop and some from Warmwell. Contact had been made with the enemy especially by 609 operating from the satellite and by No 501 (County of Gloucester) Auxiliary Squadron who had arrived on 4th July with Hurricane Is.

The first major raid on the airfield came on Thursday 8th August. On the previous evening, convoy CW9 code-named 'Peewit' had sailed from the Thames Estuary with 20 ships. As the convoy travelled through the Straits, the German radars, high on the cliffs of the Pas-de-Calais had detected the passage. At 9 am on the morning of the 8th, Stukas of Stukageschwader 2 operating from St Malo and Lannion, attacked the convoy but were beaten off by a superior number of RAF

F/O the Lord Richard Ughtred Paul Kay-Shuttleworth of No 145 Squadron of the RAFVR. Flying to defend the 'Peewit' convoy and just south of the Isle of Wight, he was involved in a dogfight with JU 87s and ME 110s. He failed to return from this sortie and was reported 'missing in action'. Neither he nor his aircraft were ever found. (Plaistow Pictorial)

fighters, the Luftwaffe losing a number of Stukas.

The convoy, virtually untouched, sailed on. Mainly colliers, they were laden with part of the 40,000 tons of coal and coke needed every week to keep industry going in the south of the country. Two destroyers had been provided by Portsmouth to act as the main escorts but the convoy should have been allocated several more to fend off the aerial attacks.

At 12.45, the bombing was resumed by 57 Stukas just as the ships were off the Isle of Wight. This time, escorted by ME 109s of JG 27 commanded by Major Max Ibel, the bombers found their mark and many ships in the convoy were hit. Many casualties were also sustained and although once again the RAF fighters from Tangmere and various other bases met the enemy over the coast, the ships that were still afloat were duly noted by the German pilots for the next attack. The raid had cost the convoy four merchant ships sunk, with seven others badly damaged. The rest struggled around the Isle of Wight and were approaching Weymouth Bay when 82 Stukas escorted by 68 ME 109s and ME 110s appeared overhead. Nos 43, 145 and 152 squadrons attacked the vast armada shooting down three Stukas and damaging four others.

This was the last raid on 'Peewit'. Late that evening the remaining ships steamed limply into Swanage harbour with only four ships undamaged. Seven had been sunk, six had been badly damaged and four of the naval escorts had also been hit. Despite their obvious success in breaking up the convoy, the Luftwaffe had suffered badly. The Middle Wallop squadrons, Nos 238 and 609 had helped in the destruction, the former claiming two ME 110s and a ME 109 destroyed with four unconfirmed kills for the loss of three aircraft of their own whilst the latter claimed three ME 110s and two JU 87 Stukas destroyed. Of the three aircraft 238 lost, F/Lt D E Turner and F/O D C MacCaw were killed. The third, Sqd/Ldr H A Fenton, was rescued from the sea by *HMS Bassett* and taken to Haslar Hospital, Gosport.

As sunset came at Middle Wallop, all the squadrons counted the cost of the 'Peewit' convoy. It was now obvious to everyone that the full might of the enemy would soon be turned upon the airfields, for without the destruction of the RAF and their airfields no invasion could take place.

The Middle Wallop squadrons were scrambled constantly over the coming days. On the 12th August, two more convoys, code-named 'Arena' and 'Agent' were the subject of many enemy attacks as they

Part of the damage caused to Middle Wallop by the 14th August raid. The doors of No 5 hangar fell in, crushing three airmen. (Plaistow Pictorial)

made their way out of the Thames Estuary. Further south at Portsmouth, two further convoys, code-named 'Snail' and 'Cable' were also receiving heavy attacks. The Luftwaffe met fierce opposition with 152 Squadron from Warmwell losing two Spitfires with both pilots listed as missing.

Tuesday 13th August, known as 'Eagle Day', was a bad day for Middle Wallop and for 238 Squadron. Whilst it was the turn of the Kent airfields to be bombed in the morning, a large formation of enemy aircraft was seen on radar to be formating over the Cherbourg peninsula shortly after 3.30 pm. A warning was received at Rudloe Manor, No 10 Group headquarters, that three formations consisting of about 90 aircraft, were crossing towards Middle Wallop and Portsmouth. AVM Brand, the commander of 10 Group, ordered 238 Squadron to be scrambled from Middle Wallop and Nos 152 and 609 squadrons from the satellite at Warmwell. Although this left both bases undefended, it was better to attack the enemy before he crossed the coast if possible.

At Middle Wallop the sirens began to wail. Airmen and women not on essential duty rushed to the new and sometimes partially completed shelters. Shortly after, JU 87 Stukas and a lone JU 88 bombed the airfield but damage was limited to an area just behind the No 238 Squadron dispersal area. In the ensuing battle, 238 lost four Hurricanes with one pilot lost, one injured and two unhurt.

The next day, a major attack was made on the airfield. Although cloudy over the Channel, Luftflotte 3 were briefed for an afternoon attack on the Southampton area. Wg/Cdr David Roberts, the sector controller at Wallop, was warned that the airfield could be a major target as a general air-raid warning was issued for the Southampton area at 5 pm. Sure enough, a group of HE 111s and JU 88s dived from the clouds and dropped bombs on the airfield. Although most of them fell wide of their mark, one JU 88 dropped a string of five bombs which hit hangars 4 and 5, an air-raid shelter, the station headquarters and sector control room. The attack took its toll with three airmen trapped beneath the heavy doors of hangar 5, they had been closing it at the time of the attack, and three civilians killed in the shelter. Three Spitfires of 609 Squadron were lost together with a similar number of Blenheims belonging to 604 Squadron. Fires burnt fiercely all around the station, this punctuated by the sound of ammunition exploding from the burning aircraft. No 609 had been airborne at the time of the attack and were patrolling Boscombe Down area when they noticed a lone JU 88 slipping in and out of the light cloud. Two Spitfires, flown by Sgt Alan Feary and F/O Dundas respectively, followed it down and coming out of cloud, saw it was attacking Middle Wallop. Although attacked by F/O Dundas earlier on it was Sgt Feary who closed on the enemy aircraft and gave it a burst of gunfire from 250 yards astern. As the JU 88 began to dive, he pumped the rest of his ammunition into it and had the satisfaction of seeing it catch fire and crash on heathland near North Charford. Three of the crew perished. Pilot Oberleutnant Wilhelm Heinricci and co-pilot Gefreiter Heinz Stark were killed outright whilst Gefreiter Freidrich Ahrens died later from his injuries and Gefreiter Eugen Sauer became a prisoner of war.

The attacks on Middle Wallop however were not over. No 609 Squadron managed to land and re-arm and re-fuel before being scrambled again at around 5.15 pm. It was just in time as a JU 88 dropped a string of bombs across the field. Some were delayed action so the impact was not immediately felt. As it disappeared into light cloud, 609 arrived on the scene and missing the JU 88, found a lone HE 111 weaving to avoid detection. P/O D Crook managed to get in a shot and damaged the aircraft as it jettisoned its bomb load over Roche

A scene typical of the Battle of Britain as a downed airman awaits his rescue by a Walrus. (S E Newspapers)

Court. It was then chased by F/O Dundas who attacked it, causing smoke to pour out of the starboard engine. Lowering its undercarriage and hoping for a flat area of land, Oberst Alois Stockel crashed his aircraft at East Dean. He died together with Oberst Georg Francke and Oberleutnant Bruno Brossler. Two other crew members, Feldwebel Heinz Grimmstein and Feldwebel Thiel were captured and marched into captivity. By nightfall the county was littered with aircraft wrecks, the majority of them German.

As the last attack ended and dusk approached, Fighter Command knew that the second phase of the battle had only just begun. They realised that worse was to come but did not expect that the next day, Thursday 15th August 1940, would see all four fighter groups in action and that it would cost both the Luftwaffe and the RAF many losses.

With a ridge of high pressure firmly established over the British Isles, the Luftwaffe proposed its greatest effort of the campaign so far. The plan was to attack on as wide a front as possible aimed at bringing most of the RAF into battle as well as wrecking the radar stations, thus denying Fighter Command any advance warning.

The morning brought several devastating attacks on the early warning radar stations in Kent and Sussex followed by raids on the airfields. (See *Sussex Airfields in the Second World War*.) In the early afternoon Kent once again took the brunt with Suffolk a close second. Middle Wallop had to wait until early evening before sirens heralded an attack on the airfield by the aircraft of Luftflotte 3, who were based in Paris under the command of Generalfeldmarschall Hugo Sperrle. Twelve JU 88s escorted by ME 110s flew very low across the airfield and dropped their bombs simultaneously. Once again, what was left of hangars 4 and 5 took the brunt of the attack together with several minor buildings. With the airfield defence guns adding to the noise of the crump, crump of bombs exploding, those on duty in the sector operations room and elsewhere wondered if they could survive such an onslaught. Although the runway was cratered from the previous raids, 609 Squadron had been scrambled shortly before the airfield was attacked. Now they returned to attack the bombers and their escorts as the enemy aircraft turned and headed home. They did well claiming one JU 88 destroyed with three probables and three ME 110 fighters destroyed, Flt/Lt MacArcher shooting down two of these. Another 110 fell to F/O Ostaszewski of 609 and P/O Zurakowski of 234 Squadron, both sharing in the victory. For the Middle Wallop sector the day saw three Spitfires of 152 Squadron lost, all three pilots surviving, four

The cockpit of a Mosquito night-fighter of No 604 Squadron, equipped with AI Mk VIII radar. The observer's cathode ray tube is clearly seen. (IWM)

Spitfires of 234 Squadron lost with one pilot killed, one unhurt and two captured by the Germans when their aircraft crashed into the Channel. Other losses were a Blenheim of 604 Squadron which was destroyed on the ground during the raid and one attacked mistakenly by P/O D M Crook of 609 Squadron. The pilot managed to crash-land the aircraft back at Middle Wallop with only slight injuries to the gunner. The Blenheim however was a total write-off and the feelings between 604 and 609 Squadrons were strained, to say the least, for some time.

The Luftwaffe put up 1,786 sorties during this 24 hour period using every type of aircraft they had. They claimed to have shot down 82 Hurricanes and Spitfires, five non-existent Curtiss Hawks and 14 unknown types. In reality the figure was 34 aircraft but unfortunately with 17 pilots killed and 16 wounded. The RAF figures when released were also somewhat incorrect claiming 182 enemy aircraft shot down over 974 sorties whereas the figure was actually 75. In the heat of a battle such as this, claims were very easily exaggerated. The German losses were far heavier than anticipated and did not produce the hoped-for results. The loss of so many aircraft brought about the removal from daylight operations of Luftflotte 5, operating from

Norway and Denmark, as many of their aircraft were transferred to Luftflotte 2 in order to increase the armada of aircraft available. The day's events also saved the early warning radar chain from further destruction as Reichmarschall Goering, in his ignorance, issued a statement saying 'It is doubtful whether there is any point in continuing the attacks on radar sites in view of the fact that not one of those attacked has so far been put out of action'. His intelligence service failed to observe that several radar stations, including Ventnor, were barely operational. It also said little for the navigational skills of the German airmen who, whilst bombing Middle Wallop, West Malling and Croydon, were under the impression they were over Andover, Biggin Hill and Kenley!

Work carried on throughout the night to repair the grass runways. The next two days saw a lull in enemy activity as the Luftwaffe regrouped its forces. The sector stations began to look at the vulnerability of the operations rooms.

At Middle Wallop this was housed in a hut and during the bombing of the 16th it came very near to total destruction. It was generally appreciated by now that ops rooms on airfields should have been underground and blast proof. Time however had not allowed that, but by mid-August, a purpose-built ops room was under construction at a less vulnerable site on the airfield.

No 238 Squadron had left Middle Wallop just prior to the Luftwaffe attacks and moved to St Eval on the Cornish coast. Likewise, No 236 had taken their Blenheims to Thorney Island on the 4th July 1940 to be replaced by No 234 (Madras Presidency) Squadron who flew their Spitfires up from St Eval on the 13th August. No 601 (County of London) Auxiliary Squadron had come and gone, 501 (County of Gloucester) Auxiliaries had moved to Gravesend during July and the end of August saw 609 (West Riding) and the aforementioned 234 Squadrons together with 604, the night-fighter squadron and 152 who were still resident at Warmwell.

On the 31st July Fighter Command took its heaviest losses with 39 aircraft lost and 14 pilots killed. Whilst the German attacks were still mainly concentrated on the airfields, there were no further heavy raids for Middle Wallop. By November the tactics had changed. It was now London that became the main target together with most of the other large cities. Attacks by night became more commonplace including some further large scale raids on Fighter Command airfields. Night navigation was difficult and in order to confuse the enemy, a dummy

107

airfield for Middle Wallop was built at Broughton. A mobile generator was used to supply power to a simulated flare-path and various other points around the fake airfield. Known as a 'Q' site, the dummy saved Middle Wallop on several occasions from further destruction.

As the raids changed to nights, No 604 (County of Middlesex) Squadron began to come into its own. It had arrived at Middle Wallop in July 1940 under the command of Sqd/Ldr M F Anderson and was equipped with the Bristol Blenheim IF, which as a night-fighter was wholly ineffective. The main problem was that they were too slow to catch any enemy aircraft but also they had no airborne radar with which to intercept them. As autumn approached, little black boxes were put into the Blenheims and words like 'airborne interception' began to be banded about. Scientists arrived to busy themselves in the aircraft, fiddling knobs and fine tuning a pattern on a screen. It was all very mysterious!

Yet it was hoped that the little black boxes contained the answer to the night-fighters' prayers and that it would assist in the destruction of the enemy by night.

604 Squadron had within its ranks a pilot destined to become one of the aces of night-fighting. Flt/Lt John Cunningham, promoted to command 'B' flight of 604 in September 1940, was soon to acquire the detested nickname of 'Catseyes'. He was so called to deprive the enemy of any knowledge of airborne radar, his rapidly increasing tally of enemy aircraft being attributed to his consumption of carrots which improved his eyesight to the perfection of a cat's. It was however with the conversion to the Bristol Beaufighter in late October that he and many other pilots really got to down the enemy in considerable numbers.

The Beaufighter offered both speed and fire-power to deliver attacks on the Luftwaffe at night. Its airborne radar was a great improvement on the set installed in the Blenheims and with the assistance of Donald Parry, a civilian scientific officer who came to Middle Wallop as the aircraft arrived, 604 Squadron soon entered a period of classroom conversion to the new apparatus.

The first kill for the squadron took place on the 20th November 1940 when John Cunningham and his observer John Phillipson were airborne from Middle Wallop. They were vectored onto an enemy aircraft and upon switching on his airborne radar, John Phillipson got an immediate contact. With the blip holding firm on his cathode ray tube, he was able to bring them into close range. Straining his eyes,

John Cunningham stared ahead and saw a vague shape beginning to form. Climbing a fraction higher he saw a distinctive outline and shouted to his observer 'OK, I can see it'. At last the enemy was no longer invisible as John fired his guns and had the satisfaction of seeing a JU 88 plunging to earth. 604 Squadron from Middle Wallop had shot down the first enemy aircraft with a Beaufighter using airborne radar.

Next morning the press flocked to Middle Wallop and the nickname that John and many others detested was born.

On the 21st September the Luftwaffe returned to bomb the airfield. One oil and four incendiary bombs were dropped on the boundary near the ops room with six high-explosive bombs landing near the officers mess. The single JU 88 of Lehrgeschwader 1 operating from Orleans/Bricy was caught by a Spitfire of 234 Squadron and made to force-land in Sussex. Oblt Sodemann, Fw Bergstrasser, Fw Lorenz and Gefr Bossert were all captured and their aircraft was a write-off.

By the end of the Battle of Britain, the Middle Wallop sector had considerably expanded, supporting No 238 Squadron at Chilbolton and No 56 (Punjab) Squadron at Boscombe Down. Both squadrons flew Hurricanes. A detachment (D) of 23 Squadron with Blenheims paid a brief visit during September returning to Ford in Sussex on the 25th of the month. The days of 609 Squadron were numbered and after a very successful period at Middle Wallop, they finally left for the satellite at Warmwell on the 29th November. As autumn approached, the longer nights meant good hunting for the Beaufighters of 604 who continued to achieve success. The CO, Mike Anderson, shot down a HE 111 a few nights after John Cunningham's success aided by a new secret control radar called GCI, (Ground Controlled Interception). The system involved a mobile radar caravan packed with equipment which allowed a fighter controller to vector a night-fighter to within yards of an enemy aircraft. It was then that the airborne radar in the Beaufighter would take over so that the observer could guide his pilot to the final kill. Although the system was still in its experimental stage, the first results were very encouraging.

The autumn and winter of 1940/41 gave a spell of very clear, crisp nights, with the enemy taking full advantage of them. Each night, just before dusk, aircraft of 604 would be scrambled and in December, John Cunningham and his observer destroyed two Heinkels even before nightfall had really arrived.

The new GCI stations were springing up all over the south-east, the closest to Middle Wallop being at Sopley and code-named 'Starlight'.

A Douglas Havoc of No 538 Turbinlite Squadron. Though a good idea, it failed dismally in practice. (RAF Museum)

Others often controlled 604 including Tangmere (Boffin) and Foreland (Skyblue). There developed a certain rapport between the pilots and the controllers seated in their draughty caravans sometimes miles from nowhere, for in order to shoot down the enemy teamwork was essential.

Sunday 6th October 1940 saw the return of the Luftwaffe to Middle Wallop when a loan raider dropped three high-explosive and one oil bomb in the north-west corner of the airfield. Little damage was done and no casualties were reported.

With the coming of November and December, Middle Wallop entered a period of experimental flying. On the 7th December 1940, No 93 Squadron re-formed at the base from No 420 Flight equipped with the Handley Page Harrow. Employed on night-fighter duties, the Harrow was really totally unsuitable for this type of work, having originally been designed as a twin engined bomber as far back as 1937. Never used operationally in this role, it was relegated to training bomber crews but during the winter blitz of 1940/41, the bomber was used in a rather bizarre operation code-named 'Operation Mutton'.

No 93 Squadron came to Middle Wallop to take part in the operation. The unit was formed to develop a system of laying a line of small mines suspended on 2,000 ft of piano wire which was then suspended from a 36 inch diameter parachute and dropped from a Harrow in front or across an approaching enemy bomber force. Theoretically, an enemy aircraft would then fly into the suspended wire, catching it on its wing

110

whereupon the mine would be pulled up to explode on the wing root. The first successful curtain was laid by 93 Squadron on 22nd November when 160 mines were laid by a single Harrow. It did however present problems when some mines exploded prematurely causing a tear in the aircraft's fabric and making it difficult to control. Despite this and other problems, the idea was passed as acceptable and due to the age and sluggish manoeuvrability of the Harrow, 22 Douglas Havoc Mk I aircraft were converted to carry Long Air Mines (LAM). The name Havoc was first applied to the RAF night-fighter and night intruder versions of the Douglas Boston in 1940. American-built, over 100 aircraft were converted to Havocs by the Burtonwood Aircraft Repair Depot near Liverpool with 93 Squadron receiving 20 aircraft. These were further modified to carry the aerial mines in the bomb bay, the entire conversion being known as the 'Pandora', as in 'Pandora's box'.

There is no record of this idea ever succeeding in downing an enemy aircraft. It did in fact prove a considerable danger both to aircrews and civilians alike. Imagine the thoughts of a lady in Salisbury who awoke one morning to find one of the mines hanging on her washing line! Or the Amesbury policeman who, having found some mines hanging from trees, retrieved them and jauntily swinging them about his head, took them to his local station. When everyone realised just what they were the area was cleared in seconds to await the RAF bomb disposal team!

By June 1941 it had become obvious that the mine dropping idea was of little value and besides, the increased effectiveness of the Beaufighters of 604 and other squadrons ensured that the enemy was being shot down at night in ever-increasing numbers. There was however, one more experimental unit to be formed at Middle Wallop in the shape of the Turbinlite Flight.

Again it was formed as part of 93 Squadron but with the imminent demise of the LAM Flight, the Havocs were used as airborne searchlights known as the Helmore Turbinlites. Very strong battery powered searchlights were installed in the nose of the aircraft and the wide and intense beam of light produced was intended to illuminate an enemy aircraft picked up by the Havoc's airborne radar. An accompanying aircraft, usually a Hurricane, would then attempt to shoot down the enemy.

In October 1941 No 1458 Flight was created from a nucleus of 93 Squadron and thus became a separate unit under the command of

Sqd/Ldr C R Stuart. Earlier in the year No 32 Squadron had brought their Hurricane Is in from Acklington and although intended to be used in conjunction with the Turbinlite Squadron, departed to Ibsley, now another satellite of Middle Wallop, on the 16th February 1941. This departure heralded the return of 238 Squadron from Chilbolton but they too went back there on the 1st February.

A new type of aircraft arrived at Middle Wallop on the 6th February 1941 when a detachment of No 256 Squadron brought its Boulton Paul Defiant Is in from Colerne. The Defiant was notable as the first RAF fighter in squadron service with a four-gun turret instead of the usual forward firing guns. The first major action with the type was on 12th May 1940 when No 264 Squadron found that the turret paid handsome dividends. By 31st May they had shot down 65 enemy aircraft, a record for any type of fighter. This was mainly over Dunkirk when the power-operated turret caught the Luftwaffe by surprise. They soon however recovered and realising that the turret could not fire downwards, attacked the aircraft from underneath. As a result of this, its fame was shortlived and many were shot down. It became no match for the forward firing guns of the Luftwaffe fighters and with losses continuing at an unacceptable rate, the Defiant was withdrawn from front line service by August 1940. It did however have a resurgence of fame in the long nights of 1940/41 when it reverted to a successful night-fighter role.

After a cold and frosty winter, Middle Wallop looked forward to a better season of hunting. No 1458 Flight were still working up to operational standard with their Turbinlite Havocs, the detachment of No 256 Squadron continued operating the Defiant in a limited night-fighter role but 604 Squadron still led the night offensive. Although by this time the daylight battle had dwindled considerably, there was a vast increase in night attacks. In addition to the GCI stations, several radar beacons had been established around which night-fighters would hold until called by the controller to commence an attack. In that way, several aircraft would already be airborne and therefore able to reach the enemy aircraft more quickly.

Leading the squadron at this time in the number of kills was John Cunningham. He and his new observer Jimmy Rawnsley made an unbeatable team, resulting in the award of a DSO to John, already the holder of a DFC, and of the DFM to Jimmy in March 1941. Middle Wallop was honoured about that time by a visit from King George VI. All three squadrons were on parade as His Majesty walked down the long line of aircrew. Stopping at Jimmy Rawnsley, he asked him his score. 'Er — nine Sir,' replied Jimmy.

'Nine eh,' replied the king, 'will you get another one tonight for me?'

'Well Sir, I will certainly try my best,' came the reply.

One hour later, John and Jimmy were airborne under the control of Starlight (Sopley GCI). Calling the aircraft, the controller gave them a vector to steer. At the same time the crew were informed that the king was in the GCI control room.

'Vector (steer) three three zero,' the controller instructed and then, 'three one zero'. Jimmy Rawnsley watched the cathode ray tube in his position intently. 'Three six zero, you are three miles behind him now John,' came the controller. Suddenly a blip appeared on the screen. 'Contact,' shouted Jimmy. John reported this to the Starlight controller and skillfully gained speed on the enemy aircraft. With the contact appearing stronger John saw his target dead ahead. Coming up just under the aircraft they recognised it as a Heinkel. With a crash of his guns, John saw a flicker of flame appear on the fuselage and seconds later they both had the satisfaction of seeing it plunge to earth. Another kill to 604 Squadron and a bonus for the king who witnessed the entire episode.

1941 proved a particularly bad time with further attacks on Middle Wallop. On the 8th April, nine bombs were dropped in a field close by with incendiaries landing in the area of 93 Squadron's dispersal but with no serious damage. At 11.50 the next night five bombs were dropped on the flarepath and in the early hours of the 10th, two high-explosive bombs landed near a billet with another two close by No 4 hangar, which suffered slight damage, and one Beaufighter of 604 Squadron was hit. Seven bombs on the 16th April damaged a Blenheim and three Beaufighters with yet again a hit on No 4 hangar. The last sizeable attack came on the 12th May at 12.20 am when 12 bombs were dropped but caused little damage. Middle Wallop was still very much on the Luftwaffe agenda!

As the spring progressed, the role of the squadrons at the airfield began to change from defence to attack. Middle Wallop grew as further land was requisitioned. From 1941 onwards the Air Ministry ruled that all operation rooms should be moved some distance away from the operational airfields. Once again the sector ops room moved from the standard building on the corner of the airfield to Wallop House, a large family mansion in nearby Nether Wallop. The grounds of the house became a multitude of Nissen huts as accommodation for the ops room personnel was constructed and the old ballroom of the house became the central operations room. Even this was really only a temporary measure as the entire operation was to move to a purpose built complex later in the war.

1941 also saw No 245 (Northern Rhodesia) Squadron bring their Hurricane IIBs to Middle Wallop from Chilbolton, now an airfield in its own right and not just a satellite. They began offensive sweeps over France as the war changed to an offensive one. No 604 were still operating at night and had already reached the magical score of 30 by May 1941. In August, John Cunningham was promoted to Wg/Cdr and appointed CO of 604 Squadron as Wg/Cdr C H Appleton DSO DFC was moved to a staff job. Several Norwegians arrived at the squadron to train for night-fighters, beginning an association that was to last until the end of the war. They, together with the rest of the officers, were billeted some distance away from Middle Wallop at the Pheasant Inn, a fine old coaching station on the road to Salisbury. This was the ideal place for relaxation after a night's flying. As was the custom then, part of the ceiling was used to write names in candle-wax or to leave a sooty footprint for posterity. Christmas and New Year were celebrated at the Pheasant for those not on duty as 604 and the other squadrons at Middle Wallop looked forward to the coming of spring and another year closer to the end of the war.

1942 was the year of offensive duties as the RAF continued to carry the war back to the Continent. No 1458 Flight were still struggling with the Turbinlite Havocs, achieving little success. The Defiants of the 256 Squadron detachment had left, 245 had sent a detachment of their Hurricanes to Shoreham in Sussex but were still operating the main unit with the Turbinlite Flight combined with offensive sorties over France. They were to continue the Turbinlite operation until 26th October 1942 when they gratefully moved to Charmy Down. With very little success and a few losses through mid-air collisions with the mother aircraft, it had been a very depressing period for the squadron.

By this time both the Americans and the Japanese had entered the war but of greater significance to the British was the fact that in August 1942, Field Marshall Erwin Rommel and the British 8th Army under the command of General Montgomery stood poised, facing each other at El Alamein in Egypt. The former was re-organising his army and preparing to rush the Suez Canal whilst the latter was planning to stop Rommel in his tracks. As history records, on the 23rd October 1942, after 12 days of intense fighting, Rommel withdrew and escaped through Libya to fight another day. With Montgomery victorious, it paved the way for 'Operation Torch', the Anglo/US landings in French North Africa.

Whilst all of this had little effect on the day-to-day running of Middle Wallop, it did give everyone a feeling that the tide had turned and that victory was within sight.

Contrary to popular belief, the North American Mustang fighter was not a British version of an American aircraft. It was designed at the outset as an aircraft specifically for the European theatre of operations and only after did it enter service with the USAAF. The first Mustangs reached Britain in November 1941 but despite the plane's very good performance at lower levels, it was handicapped by a lack of power produced by the 1,150 hp Allison engine at high altitudes. Despite its high expectations, the type was only used on armed tactical reconnaissance duties instead of normal front line fighter sorties. In this role, the aircraft supplied squadrons of Army Co-operation Command although later marks of the Mustang were to become legends in long-range escort duties. One of the squadrons to receive the Mustang I was No 16. They converted to it whilst stationed at Weston Zoyland but in April 1942, a detachment arrived at Middle Wallop. These were the first Mustangs to be seen at the airfield and were the subject of much interest. They carried out shipping reconnaissance patrols in addition to normal army training exercises.

Although they did not know it, the days of 604 Squadron at Middle Wallop were numbered. They had enjoyed a very successful time at the station since the introduction of GCI and the AI equipped Beaufighters. Now they were to leave that station and move on to Predannack. Not before however, John Cunningham received another bar to his DSO and had been told that he was to take over from Rory Chisholm, another night-fighter ace, the job of directing the work of all night operational training units in Fighter Command. He and his navigator/observer Jimmy Rawnsley said goodbye to the ground-crews and after a farewell party at the Pheasant, left for pastures new. No 604 finally left Middle Wallop on the 7th December 1942, never to return.

June 1942 saw the Canadians arrive when No 44 (City of Toronto) Squadron of the RCAF deployed a detachment of Mustang Is to Middle Wallop. Although strictly a unit of the RCAF, the squadron operated under the control of the British and was effectively an RAF squadron. The detachment remained until 1st February 1943 when it moved over to Dunsfold.

One month after the first Canadian squadron had arrived, No 501 (County of Gloucester) Squadron of the Royal Auxiliary Air Force made a welcome return to Middle Wallop. The airfield had changed somewhat since the dark days of 1940 but Sqd/Ldr J W Villa DFC, the CO, could still remember how it was then. Now flying the Spitfire VC they arrived on the 24th August, left for Hawkinge on the 8th October and returned to Wallop for a brief stay on the 10th October. By the 19th they had departed to Ballyhalbert.

They were followed by No 504 (County of Nottingham) Squadron, also an auxiliary unit, who arrived from Ballyhalbert on the 19th October. Flying the Spitfire VB, they converted to the VC mark whilst at Middle Wallop. This mark of Spitfire was a fighter/bomber and could carry a single 500-lb bomb beneath the fuselage or two 250-lb bombs beneath the wings. They carried out offensive operations operating both as fighters and bombers but departed to Ibsley on the 30th December 1942.

Another squadron of the RCAF, 406 (Lynx) brought their Beaufighter VIFs in from Predannack on the 8th December. The mark VI was produced for Fighter Command fitted with an up-rated Hercules VI engine and armed with four 20 mm guns in the nose and six .303 guns in the wings. With a maximum speed of 337 mph and a range of 1,480 miles, it carried out offensive strikes over France during its three month stay at Middle Wallop.

With Christmas celebrations over, the new year brought further success for the allies. In January, Churchill and Roosevelt, together with their advisers, met for the third meeting of the war at Casablanca in Morocco. Plans were made for the opening of a second front and it was agreed that once North Africa had been cleared of the enemy, Sicily should be invaded.

Many squadrons during the war bore names of countries within their official badges just as did many auxiliary squadrons of the RAF. One reason was that some squadrons were manned by a large proportion of Commonwealth personnel, another was that aircraft of the squadron had been funded by other countries. No 164 Squadron was the Argentine/British unit; much of the funding for this squadron had come from Argentina. Equipped with the Hurricane IV, they arrived at Middle Wallop from Fairwood Common on the 8th February 1943. With the motto 'Firmly we fly', they too commenced fighter/bomber operations. The Hurricane IV was the last main production version with 1,457 of them being built in Canada. It specialised in low level attacks and was capable of withstanding a lot of punishment. No 164 used them to good effect in tank busting sorties over the Continent.

There now followed a period of even more rapid changes for the airfield. The 1st February 1943 saw No 414 (Sarnia Imperials) of the RCAF, once again with Mustang Is. In March No 19 Squadron arrived from Perranporth with Spitfire VCs, then the first Typhoons to be seen at Middle Wallop when No 182 came in from Martlesham Heath. No 247 (China/British) Squadron also flew their Typhoons in during March and yet another RCAF unit arrived on the 29th of the month when the Mosquito IIs of No 456 Squadron came in from Valley in Wales. Most of the squadrons stayed for a month or less before leaving, with the exception of 456 who under the command of Wg/Cdr M H Dwyer, stayed until August 1943.

No 1458 Turbinlite Squadron had been renumbered No 537 Squadron in September 1942. With very little success in shooting down the enemy at night, the unit disbanded on 25th January 1943. Whilst the principle had been sound, it failed to achieve anywhere near the expected results.

By June the sector operations room was once again on the move, this time to a purpose-built complex in Over Wallop. This self-contained building was to remain in use until the end of the war. As the controllers and their teams left Wallop House, it was taken over by the No 10 Group headquarters who moved over from Rudloe Manor, the site they had occupied all through the Battle of Britain.

By April the Hurricanes, Spitfires and Typhoons had left Middle Wallop. For the local populace it was a great relief that the Typhoons especially had gone for the Napier Sabre engine that powered them had proved one of the noisiest.

More Mustang Is deployed to the airfield in June when No 169 Squadron arrived from Andover. Although primarily engaged in shipping reconnaissance and ground attack missions, in July the squadron was also encountering low level attacks by enemy hit-and-run raiders. Led by Sqd/Ldr R Plumtree DFC, 169 disbanded at Middle Wallop on the 30th September and were later re-formed at Ayr.

Sicily was invaded and captured on the 10th July in 'Operation Husky'. The end of the war for Italy was fast approaching with the overthrow of Mussolini on the 25th. By September the allies had landed on the toe of Italy and one month later Italy became a friend of the allies and declared war on Germany. The news came as a tonic to all, but although victory was in sight, there was still a long way to go.

No 151 Squadron was the last to be stationed at Middle Wallop before a complete change of occupation took place. They brought their Mosquito XII night-fighters in from Colerne equipped with the new airborne interception centimetric radar. Commanded by Wg/Cdr S P Richards AFC, intruder patrols by night were carried out until November 1943 when they went back to Colerne.

From 1940 to 1943, Middle Wallop had earned a place in the history books. Now it was to close as an RAF station and become part of the United States Army Air Force. On the 12th December 1943 it was home to the 67th Reconnaissance Group and two squadrons plus several units and a headquarters formed what became known as 'Station 449'. The squadrons and units involved were Nos 12, 107 and 109 Reconnaissance Squadrons, No 30 Photo Reconnaissance Squadron and No 9 Weather Reconnaissance Squadron. Flying mainly Mustangs and Spitfires, they flew continuous sorties over the French mainland taking thousands of photographs in preparation for the invasion of France, scheduled for June 1944.

There was no respite over the Christmas period for as early as April 1943, the Americans and British had made plans for the cross-Channel invasion, code-named 'Overlord'. The greatest problem appeared to be how best to achieve surprise and prevent the enemy from knowing that the invasion would be in Normandy. Accordingly, further plans were made to convince the Germans that the landings would be along the Pas-de-Calais. Operations 'Bodyguard' and 'Fortitude' were such plans and they proved very effective in concealing the correct landing beaches. By maintaining a fake interest in Norway, thus forcing the Germans to maintain a large garrison there, and faking radio messages concerning the Pas-de-Calais region intended for German ears, the deception worked; 'Overlord' was to prove a great success and a turning point towards final victory.

Of immense help were the thousands of photos taken by the Americans from Middle Wallop. Day and night they flew reconnaissance sorties photographing every troop and tank movement, positions of guns, U-boat movements from Brest and much more. Overall command of the Allied Tactical Air Forces was given to Air Chief Marshal Sir Trafford Leigh-Mallory.

Tactical reconnaissance sorties grew until the invasion on 6th June 1944. Only after a foothold had been gained on French soil did the Americans leave Middle Wallop and by 7th July, the station had returned to the RAF.

It did not take long to re-activate the station as a new menace appeared in the skies over the UK. Hitler's long-awaited revenge weapon, the V1 or 'Doodlebug' had first been launched against the capital in the early hours of the 13th June 1944. From that time up to 200 rockets a day had been sent off from the French coast and whilst the balloon barrage and the gun sites along the south coast and around London had done sterling work in bringing many of the V1s down, the RAF was called upon to attempt to shoot them down before they even crossed the English coastline. Together with several other bases in the south and south-east, Middle Wallop was ideally situated to operate some of the 'Diver' squadrons.

On the 30th July 1944, No 125 (Newfoundland) Squadron flew in from Hurn for anti-diver operations. Flying the Mosquito XVII, a detachment was sent to Bradwell Bay in Essex to help combat V1s flying in over the east coast. One day earlier it had been the turn of another Canadian squadron to use Middle Wallop. No 418 (City of Edmonton) Squadron under the command of Wg/Cdr A Barker flew their Mosquito IIs once again in from Hurn. They only stayed a month on anti-diver operations and left for Hunsdon on the 28th August. The V1s were shot down in ever increasing numbers as the months progressed. 419 Squadron became one of the top scoring fighter squadrons in this type of operation. From July to the end of August they accounted for 90 V1s shot down out of a total of 1,979 destroyed by aircraft of the RAF. As the days shortened and the allies overran the launch sites, the number of daily firings decreased. No 125 Squadron left Middle Wallop on the 18th October and with their departure, the airfield became the home of two detachments of anti-aircraft co-operations squadrons.

Once again the Hurricane returned when a detachment of No 587 Squadron arrived in October 1944 from Weston Zoyland. Several aircraft were based around the country to undertake anti-aircraft flights with the surrounding gun batteries. A more significant arrival was No 3501 Central Servicing Unit who arrived from Cranfield in September. This was a major unit responsible for second line servicing of aircraft flown back from France. Mainly concerned with aircraft of the 2nd TAF, Middle Wallop became alive with Spitfires, Typhoons, Tempests, Mosquitos and Mustangs. This theme continued until 16th February 1945 when with victory in sight, Middle Wallop entered another stage when it was transferred to the Royal Navy and became HMS Flycatcher.

As such it was used for the administration and assembly of Mobile Naval Air Operation Bases, MONABS for short. These were mobile bases which could move onto any existing airfield and provide a suitable home for FAA aircraft that had been flown off carriers and needed shore maintenance and training facilities. Middle Wallop became the headquarters of all MONABS and saw very little flying during this period with the exception of a station flight.

Victory was celebrated at the airfield in a way fitting for a former Battle of Britain base. Six long years of war had ended and Middle Wallop had shared both triumph and despair. Now it was possible to look forward to a peaceful but uncertain future.

In preparation, the airfield was handed back to the RAF and ceased to be HMS Flycatcher on the 10th April 1946. It was immediately returned to operational status when No 165 (Ceylon) Squadron flew their Spitfire IXEs in from Duxford for five days. The 26th of the month saw the return of No 164 (Argentine/British) Squadron who had flown Hurricanes from Middle Wallop during 1943. They converted to the Spitfire LF XVIE in July and were disbanded to be renumbered No 63 Squadron in August 1946. They remained until September.

The last RAF squadron to be based at Middle Wallop was No 80 who brought the noisy Typhoon back on the 5th May 1947 but left for Wunstorf in Germany on the 16th. Before that however the airfield became a training centre for air traffic control in the south-east of England. It was the controlling airfield for the Victory fly-past over London on the 8th June 1946 and it later became the home of the Fighter Command of Control and Reporting. With No 10 Group disbanding on the 2nd May 1945, Middle Wallop became a station in the Nether Wallop sector of No 11 Group Fighter Command. Once again, the sector operations room moved back onto the station though this time into a semi-sunk bomb-proof building.

In 1996 Middle Wallop is firmly established as the major Army Air Corps airfield. Its future seems secure in a time of continual cost-cutting rounds for defence. For the aviation historian there is the superb Museum of Army Flying situated on the airfield itself and the entire site gives a nostalgic feeling of a former Battle of Britain airfield.

13
ODIHAM

Born in the lazy, hazy days of summer camps for auxiliary squadrons in 1924, it first became a landing ground for such events. It lay within easy reach of the experimental airfield at Farnborough and the army barracks at Aldershot, so with the expansion scheme of the 1930s, Odiham was a natural selection. With the acquisition of further land, the Air Ministry authorised Lindsey Parkinson Ltd to begin work on a three squadron Army Co-operation airfield. Work proceeded well and the airfield was ready for occupation by Christmas 1936. The buildings took on the usual appearance of the expansion period, i.e. neo-Georgian style officers' mess, H-block barracks, the usual station headquarters and three 'C' type hangars. Upon its completion, No 4 Squadron moved in from Farnborough with Hawker Audax aircraft on 16th February 1937. The first airmen under the command of Wg/Cdr L O Brown DFC, AFC had moved in one month earlier and with the arrival of a permanent squadron, the airfield became alive. No 4 Squadron quickly converted to the Hawker Hector, the first squadron to receive them, before they were joined by No 13 Squadron who flew in from Old Sarum. The two units specialised in night reconnaissance and carried out many exercises with local ack-ack sites. A year later they were joined by No 53 Squadron who flew their Hectors in from Farnborough to form No 50 (AC) Wing. One problem experienced with Odiham was the lack of drainage through the grass. After particularly heavy rainfalls, the airfield became unusable. Whilst this did not hamper peace-time flying, the obvious threat of war with Germany and the fact that No 53 Squadron were to receive the heavier twin-engined monoplane bomber, the Bristol Blenheim IV, it became obvious that a

121

The Westland Lysander, nicknamed Lizzie and the workhorse of all Army Co-operation Squadrons. (C. Bowyer)

hard runway would be required. Thus Odiham became the first airfield to receive a concrete runway in the south-east.

With 53 Squadron converted to the Blenheim, Nos 4 and 13 converted to the Westland Lysander. Known throughout the RAF as the 'Lizzie', the Lysander, although primarily intended for Army Co-operation duties, found fame later in the war when it was used on clandestine operations to drop agents in France. The aircraft first entered service with No 16 Squadron at Old Sarum later in 1939 but by September 1939, No 16 together with the Odiham based Lysander squadrons had moved into France to form the air component of the BEF. No 53 Squadron were also on the move and they moved to Plivot in France on 18th September 1939.

Odiham was not empty for long as two auxiliary squadrons arrived. No 613 (City of Manchester) flew their Hawker Hinds in from Ringway on the 2nd October 1939 together with No 614 (County of Glamorgan) Squadron who were still flying Lysanders.

Since the outbreak of war on 3rd September, additional personnel had been drafted into Odiham. With the airfield now on a war footing, camouflage was hastily applied to the majority of the buildings. It was

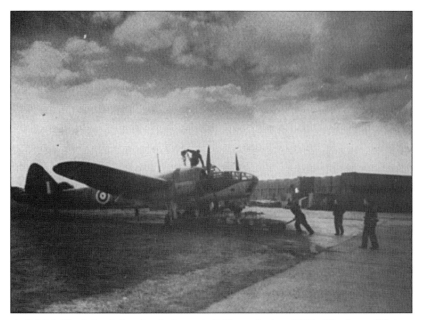

A Bristol Blenheim being bombed-up at Odiham during 1941. The large 'C' type hangars are plainly visible. (Hampshire Record Office)

planned that a decoy airfield should be built at Froyle, just three miles to the south of Odiham, lest the Luftwaffe should decide to attack what was not a fighter airfield but an Army Co-operation one.

On the 3rd October 1939, 'B' Flight of 614 Squadron was redesignated No 614A and became No 225 Squadron eight days later. Although primarily formed to aid local searchlight and ack-ack sites, the Lysanders also began flying coastal patrols along the Hampshire coast as far as the Isle of Wight and also participated in some ASR work. Working alongside, 613 Squadron were tasked with the job of ferrying reinforcement Lysanders to Amiens-Glisy to provide extra artillery spotting.

As the Battle of Britain raged overhead, not a lot of changes were made at Odiham. No 225 left for Old Sarum on 9th June 1940, 613 for Netherthorpe on 29th June and 614 for Grangemouth on 8th June.

With the fall of France and the evacuation of the BEF, No 59 Squadron flew their Blenheim bombers from Crecy-en-Ponthieu via Lympne and Andover to Odiham. They brought with them tales of

An Airspeed Oxford T1 of No 8 Flying Training School at Odiham. (MAP)

heroism and bravery in the face of the enemy onslaught and in retaliation for the defeat of the BEF, the squadron now bombed the enemy-held harbours in France. They remained at Odiham for three weeks before moving down to Thorney Island to continue the bombing. (See *Sussex Airfields in the Second World War*.)

One day after the Dunkirk evacuation, the brave Belgian people were forced to surrender to German aggression and on 10th June, Italy declared war on the Allies and promptly invaded southern France. With the downfall of mainland Europe, many Belgian, Dutch and French airmen arrived in Britain to give their services to the RAF. No 1 Fighter Training School was formed at Odiham for the Free French, equipped with a vast selection of obsolete liberated aircraft. Farmar 222s, Cauldron Goelands, Potez 63/11, Block 151s and Dewoitine 520s were suddenly descending on the airfield. Being both fighters and bombers, the aircraft were flown to England to ensure they did not fall into German hands. Certain numbers of all these types were however captured by the Luftwaffe and used against the Allies. Shortly after their arrival the French airmen were visited by General De Gaulle and the decision was made not to base these units permanently at Odiham and they were soon dispersed elsewhere.

On 10th August 1940, the Luftwaffe made an appearance over

124

Odiham. German activity on this particular day was limited to shipping and coastal reconnaissance. During one of the latter sorties, several enemy aircraft flew over but no attempt was made to attack the airfield nor any attempt by the local ack-ack units to shoot the enemy down. Two days later however, the war was to begin for Odiham.

The movement of a high pressure ridge over the Azores indicated a period of fine days for the UK. Across the Channel, Luftflotten 2 and 3 were briefed for attacks on the fighter airfields and the coastal radar stations. The first attack came at 9 am when five radar stations were attacked simultaneously. After an hour's respite, a formation of JU 87 Stukas attacked two convoys, code-named 'Arena' and 'Agent', in the Channel. At the same time JU 88s from Luftflotte 3 approached the Southampton and Portsmouth area. Whilst these towns were being bombed, another force of JU 88s attacked the Chain Home radar station at Ventnor causing serious damage and many fires. In addition to these raids, the JU 88s of KG 51 had been briefed to attack Odiham. As they crossed the coast the leading crew looked ahead and inland for a first sighting of the airfield. As they did so, No 43 Squadron operating from Tangmere, threw their Hurricanes into the attack. Caught by surprise, many of the enemy planes jettisoned their bombs and turned for home. In the space of a few minutes, over eight JU 88s fell from the sky with several more making for the Channel trailing smoke. In the fight, 43 Squadron lost just two Hurricanes with both pilots safe but this action had prevented any bombs from falling on Odiham.

Three days later the Luftwaffe returned and bombed Odiham in mistake for nearby Andover! The attack came in the early evening after a day of constant fighting by the RAF. JU 88s of LG1 with a fighter escort of ME 110s first attacked Middle Wallop and then made for Odiham thinking it to be Andover. As they approached the airfield, local ack-ack units began firing at the raiders and they were also harassed by the Hurricanes of 151 Squadron and the Spitfires of 152 Squadron. Most of the bombs dropped far too early, landing harmlessly around the perimeter before the aircraft turned for home. The Luftwaffe suffered badly again on this particular day losing 25 aircraft in all. During the 24 hour period they had put up 1,786 sorties of which 520 were bombers. This had been one of the major assaults on the airfields but it had failed to destroy the RAF.

Odiham had not really suffered at all. Some bombs had exploded in the woods around the airfield but the main runways and buildings had received no hits at all. Life carried on as usual.

125

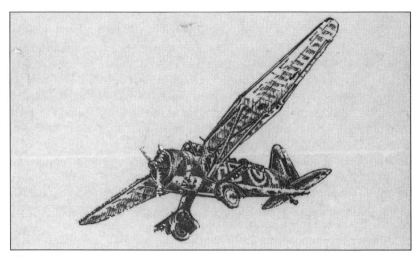

The Westland Lysander. (C Samson)

Like the Free French, the Franco-Belgian FTS formed at Odiham on 2nd November 1940. Twelve Magisters together with Lysanders and Blenheims formed the flying side of the elementary flying school. Day after day the circuit was busy with aircraft, all of them an easy target for the Luftwaffe. For whatever reason, no further attacks were made despite the trails of the dogfights to be seen all over the sky.

Towards the end of 1940 the RAF reviewed its Army Co-operation role. On 1st December 1940 the new Army Co-operation Command was formed with its headquarters at Bracknell. At the same time it was decided to replace the slow and ageing Lysander with fighter aircraft capable of photo reconnaissance work. The American-built P40 Curtiss Tomahawk was chosen to succeed the Lysanders and with this decision came a substantial upgrading of Odiham. This work commenced shortly after Christmas 1940 with the relaying of the runways and the additional provision of a tarmac perimeter track connecting the hard-standing to the runway.

The new year brought very little change to the airfield. Something of a surprise attack took place on 23rd March 1941 when a lone JU 88 hurriedly jettisoned its bombs whilst being pursued by a Hurricane. Unfortunately he chose to release them in the sky above Odiham and 12 bombs landed within the vicinity of the accommodation blocks. Very little damage was done although the incident forced everyone to

126

take to the shelters. Three days later another JU 88 flew low over the runways and was attacked by the airfield defences. No bombs were dropped, it appeared as though the Luftwaffe had forgotten about Odiham.

No 400 (City of Toronto) Squadron of the RCAF formed at Odiham from the old No 110 Squadron on 1st March 1941. Equipped initially with the Lysander, it sent detachments to Redhill and Gatwick before converting to the Tomahawk one month later. In RAF service, the Tomahawk I was powered by a 1,090 hp Allison V-1710-C15 engine. The aircraft were shipped to England in crates and re-assembled over here superseding all the Lysanders in Army Co-operation service by summer 1941. Whilst not excelling as a fighter, the aircraft proved a very good platform for low level reconnaissance work and 400 Squadron used it to its best advantage.

The new runways were extended even further in May 1941 as Odiham transferred to No 71 Group. No 13 Squadron returned from Hooton Park on 14th July 1941. Though still flying Lysanders, they quickly converted to the Blenheim IV and in addition to the usual co-operation with local units, low level bombing, gas spraying and the laying of smoke-screens were regularly practised in the sky above Hampshire.

Whilst 400 Squadron gathered experience during the winter of 1941/42, No 13 were accelerated to the dizzy heights of Bomber Command. This came about because in early 1941, the British had two concerns over bombing. One was that the command had insufficient aircraft with which to hit the enemy really hard and the second was that there was some doubt as to whether the aircraft sent on these missions actually ever hit their intended target. The addition of the camera carried on bombing raids proved conclusively that very few did. The RAF began to press for more intense raids with many more aircraft covering a wider area and thus hitting the immediate target some-where along the line. Churchill was less enthusiastic but in 1942, a new man arrived at Bomber Command.

Arthur 'Bomber' Harris was dedicated to the belief that saturation bombing would bring an early end to the war but only if he had enough aircraft. With new navigational and bombing aids being fitted to aircraft all the time, he proposed the first raid with 1,000 bombers to be launched at the end of May. The target was the German city of Cologne.

Included in this formidable bombing force was No 13 Squadron from

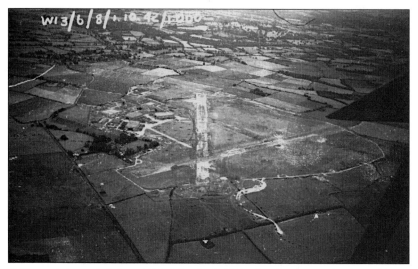

Odiham photographed from 1000 ft by the RAF in October 1942. Clearly visible are signs of the extended runways. (RAF Museum)

Odiham. Joining many other No 2 Group Blenheims, they initially carried out diversionary intruder raids but for the second raid they were briefed to bomb Bremen, another city of great importance. With a security clamp-down on the airfield, briefing was carried out in a locked room for the crews taking part. Out on the field the aircraft were bombed up and checked out by the ground-crews. As dusk fell the crews walked to their respective aircraft and formated with the other squadrons just over the North Sea. The target was found to be covered in a haze but all the aircraft dropped their bombs over a wide area and turned for home. No 13 Squadron lost one aircraft when it was shot down on the Dutch/German border. The raid was later hailed as a great success and led to many more saturation bombings.

As the summer of 1942 approached, new squadrons began to arrive. More Tomahawks came with No 171 Squadron flying in from Gatwick on the 12th July 1942. They were soon joined by No 614 (County of Glamorgan) Squadron who brought their Blenheim IVs back to Odiham from Macmerry. They found a vastly different airfield from that which they had left in 1939, then it was just going onto a war footing, now three years later it was at war. The squadron converted to the Blenheim V during August 1942 sending detachments to Weston

Zoyland and Snailwell. The V mark was the last Blenheim to enter service with the RAF. Because of its poor performance it proved very disappointing to 614 Squadron and all others that operated the type. Despite this the squadron used it to its best and attacks on airfields in the Low Countries proved successful.

With the arrival of the WAAFs at Odiham in January 1942, more accommodation was needed. As a temporary measure until further barrack blocks could be built, a large Queen Anne house in Odiham High Street, known as the 'Priory', was requisitioned. The girls were employed on duties in the operations room, SHQ and for catering. With their arrival at Odiham, suddenly life seemed so much better for the airmen!

'Operation Jubilee', the invasion of Dieppe and the hoped-for new foothold on European soil, was a total disaster. It was a period in which the Canadian Army lost more men as prisoners of war than they did in the rest of the European campaign. Originally planned to take place in early July, 'Jubilee' was postponed on two occasions due to the lack of long-term training which would have enabled the operation to be a success. Such was the lack of confidence in the assault that General Montgomery, the GOC South Eastern Command, had advised that the landings should be cancelled. One similar operation code-named 'Rutter' had already been cancelled but the Combined Operations had worked to have the plan revived and so by mid-July, it was all on again, this time using the code-name 'Jubilee'.

In the event it was not until 19th August that the invasion began. At 4.50 am a large force of naval vessels and transports arrived off pre-selected points of the French coast. It soon became clear during the raid that the enemy had forewarning of the attack and had sent additional men and armour to the area. Dieppe was not to be the easy task that so many people thought.

At Odiham, both 400 and 171 Squadrons had been flying 'Rhubarbs', low level strike operations, against enemy targets for some time. This 'softening up' process consisted of the Tomahawks straffing (machine-gunning) any likely targets such as railway installations, convoys, gun emplacements or known fuel dumps. Once the date of 'Jubilee' became known to the squadron commanders, an even bigger effort was made to lower the morale of the enemy by constant bombardment.

On the 19th August, the day of the Dieppe landings, No 400 were the first airborne from Odiham. They carried out reconnaissance sorties in addition to further straffing of the enemy. Both squadrons, together with other RAF units, covered the landings themselves and sadly witnessed some of the carnage that was going on below them. As dusk fell on the 19th, a feeling of despair was apparent as the airmen were released from duty for that day.

Dieppe however was not a total disaster for many lessons were learnt that would assist the D-Day landings when they took place in June 1944. In addition, many German heavy guns along the coastline were shattered, many ammunition dumps had been destroyed and most of all, the landings had proved that it was possible in the most heavily defended areas of German occupation to put allied troops ashore. From this moment on, plans were being made for such a landing and the ultimate invasion of the French coast.

With Dieppe over, No 171 returned to Gatwick with No 13 converting to the Blenheim V in preparation for 'Operation Torch', the invasion of French North Africa. No 400 Squadron had in the meantime converted to the North American Mustang I, the latest Army Co-operation aircraft. In addition to photographing targets in enemy occupied France, they also attacked ground targets and moved to Dunsfold in December 1942. Prior to their departure, No 168 Squadron had flown into Odiham from Bottisham on 18th November. They too immediately converted to the Mustang I.

Another Army Co-operation squadron also arrived on 18th November, this being No 239. Staying less than a month, they took their Tomahawks to Hurn and were replaced by No 174 (Mauritius) Squadron. Newly formed at Manston in Kent on 3rd March 1942, they brought the first Hurricanes to be seen at Odiham. Employed on fighter/bomber missions, the aircraft were capable of carrying either two 250 lb bombs or one 500 lb bomb. They attacked enemy shipping and coastal targets achieving some success in this role.

Christmas 1942 was celebrated in the usual style at Odiham although operations were continuous throughout the period. With the 'Torch' landings in November a great success, coupled with the Soviet counter offensive at Stalingrad the same month, it was felt by all that a little celebration would not be unreasonable.

In the light of many recent successes, 1943 opened with the Anglo/US conference at Casablanca in which Mr Churchill and President Roosevelt, together with their advisers, were to formulate the next step. The end of the month saw the German 6th Army surrender at Stalingrad and nearer home, General Montgomery was pursuing Rommel across Libya and into Tunisia.

Meanwhile another Hurricane squadron had arrived at Odiham on 14th January 1943. With the motto of 'Stop at Nothing', this is exactly what No 175 Squadron did as they commenced cross Channel sweeps in the form of 'Rhubarbs'. This was a period of rapid change for Odiham for by March, both Hurricane squadrons had moved to new bases to be replaced by further Mustangs. The arrival of Nos 170 and 268 Squadrons in June and May respectively to join No 168 meant that Odiham was now an all-Mustang base. More of the type arrived in August 1943 when No 2 Squadron flew in from Gravesend in Kent. Prior to their arrival, Odiham and all the squadrons based there had transferred to Fighter Command with No 123 Airfield headquarters being set up in tented accommodation. The headquarters controlled the operations of all the Mustang squadrons on the airfield but the task was to remain the same, that of tactical reconnaissance.

An even greater change to the air force was to take effect during 1943 when the centralised control of all air activity was announced. This was in preparation for an allied invasion to take place sometime during 1944 but for this period, a start was to be made in building up a tactical air force. The 1st June 1943 saw the disbandment of Army Co-operation command as the formation of the Second Tactical Air Force (2nd TAF) began. This change also absorbed part of Fighter Command which was itself renamed the Air Defence of Great Britain, a title that it kept until 15th October 1943.

Once again there were rapid changes at Odiham. No 4 Squadron arrived on 7th August, again from Gravesend, then on 15th September No 268 left for Funtington, an ALG in Sussex (see *Sussex Airfields in the Second World War*), Nos 168 and 170 departed on 20th September and Nos 2 and 4 Squadrons on 15th November. For the first time in many years, Odiham lay deserted of any squadrons. Somewhere, someone had decided that Odiham should for the rest of the year become a Forward Repair Unit. No 511 FRU moved in shortly after various types of aircraft arrived for repair.

1943 ended on a high note with Italy declaring war on its old ally, Germany, and the new year continuing the victory trend with the allied landings at Anzio. December 1943 saw two Typhoon squadrons arrive for attacks on 'Noball' sites. Nos 181, with its very apt motto of 'We rush in and destroy', and No 274 (China/British), both of them coming over from the Sussex ALG of Merston. The squadrons were now part of the 2nd TAF and were initially tasked with attacking the V1 rocket sites before operations connected with the D-Day landings began. They stayed three weeks before flying back to Merston.

The return of No 400 (City of Toronto) Squadron, RCAF on 18th February 1944 brought the sound of the Spitfire XI to Odiham. Briefly joined by the Typhoons of No 184 Squadron, both units flew sorties in preparation for the forthcoming invasion. As the build-up continued, Nos 168, 414 (Swordfish) and 430 (City of Sudbury) Squadrons, the latter two Canadian units, moved into Odiham to form No 128 Airfield of No 83 Group, 2nd TAF. Spitfires, Typhoons and Mustangs now flew side by side and the entire area around the airfield echoed to the sounds of aero engines both day and night.

As the rush to D-Day progressed, the airfield became No 128 Wing on 15th May. Security was of the utmost importance and Odiham was closed to outside contact. Packed with aircraft and personnel, it soon became obvious to all that invasion was near.

June 1944 came in with a period of bad weather, grounding most of the aircraft. Thanks to several deceptions on our side of the Channel, the German commanders in France believed that a major landing was to be made along the Pas-de-Calais region. These deceptions proved so effective that Field Marshal Karl von Rundstedt told his troops 'as yet there is no immediate prospect of an invasion'.

And so it was fortunate that on the eve of D-Day, arranged for 4th June, the Germans were off their guard. With foul wet weather in the Channel, the enemy felt safe along the French coast. At 4.45 am on Sunday 4th June, the landings were postponed for 24 hours due to the atrocious weather. At 9.30 pm, the Allied commanders met again and were told that a 48 hour break in the weather was coming. D-Day was rescheduled for 6th June.

At Odiham, the crews were weary of being brought to readiness and then stood down again. The signal that D-Day was on was welcomed by all as the entire 128 Wing was brought to full readiness. The battle fell into three phases. First was the breaking of the Atlantic Wall, second the army's push inland and the third the successful planning to beat off the expected counter-attack by the Germans. In all three phases, the allied aircraft were overhead. During the night of the 5th and on D-Day itself, over 14,000 sorties were flown for the loss of 127 aircraft with 63 more damaged.

At first light, aircraft from Odiham were airborne attacking enemy troops ahead of the advancing allies and carrying out tactical reconnaissance sorties. This pattern continued for many days and nights stopping only because of bad weather. Four Mustangs of No 430

Even Hampshire was not immune from the V1 attacks. The sinister shape seen above Hampshire. (IWM)

Squadron were caught in a dogfight with FW 190s for the loss of one aircraft. There were other casualties but by the end of the week it could confidently be said that along with many other bases, Odiham had contributed magnificently to the success of the landings.

With the rapid advance of the allies, 430 Squadron moved onto the Continent to B8/Sommervieu airfield on 29th June followed by 168 and 400 although the latter left a detachment of Mosquitos at Odiham. For a short time silence once again reigned but with the increased activities of No 511 FRU, and the arrival of No 130 Wing from Gatwick, it soon became business as usual.

The 27th June saw No 2 Squadron arrive briefly before flying on to B10/Plumetot followed by No 268 (Chippeway Indian) Squadron who stayed just over one month before flying to the airstrip in France. Once again the airfield seemed deserted although the landing of occasional bombers in distress made a welcome change. With D-Day over a new menace appeared in the skies in the shape of the V1 Doodlebug.

Although the majority of the rockets came in over the Kent and Sussex coastline, some did stray and cross Hampshire. To combat this new menace, 96 Squadron were posted to Odiham on 24th September 1944. Bringing their Mosquito XIIIs across from Ford, where they had been very successful in shooting down the robots, they did very little at Odiham and spent a frustrating three months in Hampshire.

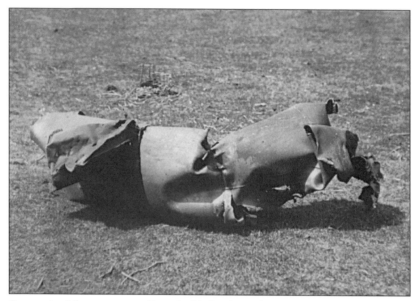

Soon parts of the county were littered with the pieces of Doodlebugs lying around in the fields. (SE Newspapers)

The FRU disbanded in December 1944 and the remnants moved onto the Continent. No 604 (County of Middlesex) Squadron arrived on 4th December for a month before taking their Mosquitos to B51/Lille airstrip. Whilst at Odiham they shot down a JU 88 over Holland, one of many that were falling to the prowling Mosquitos of the RAF. No 264 (Madras Presidency) Squadron spent three weeks at Odiham before they too departed to B51/Lille airstrip leaving No 1516 (Blind Approach Training Flight) with Airspeed Oxfords in residence.

Unfortunately the new year brought very little change and it was not until April 1945 that the airfield once again became busy as POWs returning home flew in. On 7th June Odiham was transferred from Fighter Command to No 46 Group Transport Command. The next day No 233 Squadron moved in with Dakotas which began flying scheduled services to and from the Continent. They were replaced by No 271 Squadron on the 30th August when they were posted to India. Still flying Dakotas, 271 carried on the same type of duties bringing back many troops to the UK.

The two mainstays of training in Hampshire. An Airspeed Oxford in the foreground with a Mk I Avro Anson behind. (MAP)

With the formal surrender of Germany on 7th May 1945, the entire country rejoiced. Winston Churchill proclaimed that 'we have never seen a greater day than this' and ended a speech in his usual manner with 'advance Britannia'. RAF Odiham joined the rest of the country in celebrating but the next day it was back to business. In October 1945, 271 Squadron left for Bradwell and Odiham was transferred to the RCAF on the 21st. In flew No 437 (Husky) Squadron again with Dakotas, leaving a detachment at B56/Evere and at Croydon. A year later they were joined by No 436 (Elephant) Squadron and once again the airfield was full of Dakotas.

On 28th June 1946 the Canadians handed Odiham back to the RAF as No 11 Group Fighter Command resumed control. The Canadian squadrons left as the airfield moved into the jet era. With many other famous bases being closed as surplus to requirements, Odiham survived and was to become a major peace-time base.

14
PORTSMOUTH

Though not one of the major wartime airfields in Hampshire, Portsmouth is nonetheless worthy of a chapter. It is sad that the airport did not survive beyond 1973 but with the close proximity of Southampton Airport, it became obvious that the county could not support two civil airports, and Portsmouth was the one to die.

It was in 1924 that a forward-looking councillor saw an opportunity for a seaplane base, an international airport and a smaller general aviation airport. Though far too ambitious for the era, it did however plant a seed in the minds of Portsmouth Corporation. Five years later 275 acres at Portsea Island were earmarked for the construction of a civil airport. Building went ahead so rapidly that on 2nd July 1932, the airport was officially opened by the then Under Secretary of State for Air, Sir Philip Sassoon. Shortly after it opened it was visited by Alan Cobham's National Aviation Day display. The excitement of this visit was beyond anyone's dreams. Prior to the great day, banners were put up to advertise the event. Road signs directing people to the site were erected and the entire population of Portsmouth suddenly took an interest in aviation. On 10th August 1932 the great day arrived as Alan Cobham led his flying flotilla of aircraft into the little airport. Many people took the advantage of a first flight and were soon in love with flying. This encouraged the Corporation to push ahead with their plans to make Portsmouth a truly international airport.

The Flying Circus returned in 1933 to find a very busy scene. The Portsmouth, Southsea and Isle of Wight Aviation Co Ltd had started flying services to Shanklin and Shoreham and during March 1937, Airspeed Ltd had moved on the site. Portsmouth Airport had arrived.

Many varied types of aircraft were seen at the opening of the airport in 1932. The rather futuristic shape in the front rank seems to be attracting most interest. (Portsmouth Publishing)

Jersey Airlines began a service to the Channel Islands using De Havilland Dragons followed by the 'Western Air Express', the route being operated by International Airlines and calling at Croydon and Plymouth.

By 1934, Airspeed were in financial trouble but with instructions from the Air Ministry to proceed with a batch of 50 Airspeed Oxfords, more cash was forthcoming. In common with many other airfields in the country, Portsmouth received a contract to train Civil Air Guard pilots. Though basically run on military lines, the scheme encouraged civilian flying clubs to train pilots to a certain standard thus giving the RAF more ready-trained aircrew. Whilst the remuneration to the civil clubs was not great, for the would-be pilots it meant that they obtained their flying licence for next to nothing. Hampshire certainly had a lot of would-be pilots for by 1939, the Portsmouth Aero Club had flown more

CAG hours than any other club in the country! This period of preparation was none too soon for as the clouds of war once again gathered strength, the Air Ministry began to look at the small airfields as part of the country's defence.

Whilst it was not anticipated that Portsmouth would be a major RAF station, it was however requisitioned by the Air Ministry in September 1939 as a service and overhaul airfield. The aircraft of the flying club and the commercial companies operating from the site left but the majority of their staff stayed put with a re-organised company known as Portsmouth Aviation. In addition to the manufacturing of Oxfords by Airspeed, the new company received contracts to repair RAF aircraft.

As the Battle of Britain began, it soon became obvious that Portsmouth, although not a fighter airfield, would soon attract the Luftwaffe due to its close proximity to a major naval base. A very limited defence force consisting of three Lewis guns were placed around the perimeter of the airfield, hardly enough to fight off a major attack.

This however was exactly the plan that Hitler had in mind when he issued his Directive No 16. It dictated that in addition to detroying the RAF, it was also to attack manufacturing plants and the British naval forces at their home bases. Whilst the probing of British defences and attacks on Channel shipping began on 10th July, the first phase also included bombing raids on the dockyard. It was obvious that some of these bombs, whether intentional or not, would land on Portsmouth Airport.

Thursday 11th July 1940; a day with a cloud base of 5,000 ft and very overcast. Thunderstorms were heard in the Midlands and the north but the south-east corner stayed dry with occasional glimpses of the sun. At 7.30 am, two Luftflotte formations operating from the Cherbourg Peninsula were detected by radar heading for a convoy in Lyme Bay. The Hurricanes and Spitfires from Tangmere and Warmwell were airborne, some to cover the convoy and some to attack the enemy. Portland was the main target on this occasion but both enemy aircraft and British fighters passed very near to the airport.

Although several other raids materialised during the day, it was not until 6.10 pm that Portsmouth was subject to its first attack, carried out by aircraft of Luftflotte 3, who were detected by the early warning radar at Ventnor. Twelve HE 111s escorted by 12 ME 110s crossed over the Isle of Wight and made for the dockyard. The Hurricanes of 601 and 145 Squadrons attacked and a severe dogfight soon took place between them and the escorting 110s. Three Hurricanes were shot down with two pilots badly injured including the CO of 145 Squadron, Sqd/Ldr J R A Peel. The third aircraft landed back at Tangmere with a seized engine. Despite the RAF attack, the dockyard and Portsmouth Airport were bombed. At the latter, a string of bombs burst along the length of the grass landing area reaching the Airspeed factory. In the devastation, several workers at the factory were badly injured for it was around this time that many were going off shift and heading home. The damage to the Airspeed works could have been far worse but as it turned out, production was able to continue after two days of clearing up. Some of the design work at Airspeed was however moved away from the airfield site in the light of this attack.

The rest of July saw sporadic bombs fall around the airport but Monday 12th August saw the biggest raid on the city and surrounding area for some time. At 11.30 am a large force of JU 88s of KG 51 operating from Orly and Etampes with a heavy escort flew towards the Southampton area. Suddenly the entire defence barrage around Portsmouth opened fire, even the naval boats in the harbour fired at the enemy. As the bombs dropped, fires were started in and around the city area. On the airport yet another string was dropped across the grass but Airspeed luckily suffered no damage on this occasion. The small fires that had been started on the field were quickly extinguished by the station fire service before they raced to the city centre to help the National Fire Service with the raging fires.

As evening came, German radio claimed that several large naval ships had been sunk in the harbour and that the airfield at Portsmouth had been destroyed. They also claimed 71 RAF aircraft lost including the whole of No 65 Squadron at Manston in Kent. In fact the RAF in the course of 732 sorties had suffered 22 casualties whilst the Luftwaffe lost 31.

The next day, 'Eagle Day', saw further raids on airfields in Hampshire including Portsmouth, where serious damage was inflicted on the docks with further bombs on Airspeed. By this time the grass landing area resembled a colander but after each raid all non-essential personnel were busy filling in the craters. Throughout all of this, the Oxford production continued. Though August and September were to see many other raids on Portsmouth City and the docks area, the airfield suffered only minor attacks. With the end of the Battle of Britain, it appeared to have been forgotten and only one large raid in

Sadly Portsmouth airport soon fell into disrepair, as this 1980 photograph shows. (L Pilkington)

April 1941 took any life. Production at Airspeed was to continue unhindered for the rest of the war.

From 1943 onwards, the sight of partly assembled Horsa gliders became common as they sat silently upon the grass. Built in preparation for the D-Day landings, they were supplemented by the mighty four-engined Halifax, many of which flew into Portsmouth for use on glider towing trials. The only other aircraft seen during this period were the gliders of No 163 Gliding School used by the Air Cadets.

From 1939 to 1945, 4,411 Airspeed Oxfords were built at Portsmouth, the last one coming off the line on 14th July 1945. It was thought by many that with the war ended, there would be no further orders for the type. In fact, there were none for the basic Oxford, but a conversion to a six-seater passenger aircraft known as the Consul ensured that Airspeed not only retained its workers and their skills but also made a profit. Together with a refurbishment programme for the existing Oxfords, Airspeed survived when everyone thought it would not do so.

15
WORTHY DOWN

It is worth recording that despite the many FAA squadrons that were stationed there, Worthy Down only once fired its guns in anger. This period was around 27th May 1940, the time of the evacuation of the BEF from Dunkirk. Fighter Command was struggling to put a protective cover over the evacuation beaches but the range at which the Hurricanes and Spitfires operated would leave them little fuel to stay and give protection to the troops below. It was therefore decided that in addition to the RAF, FAA aircraft would be tasked with assisting in flying patrols over the beaches even though they were equipped with almost inadequate aircraft.

No 806 Squadron FAA had formed at Worthy Down on 1st February 1940 with eight Blackburn Skuas and four Blackburn Rocs. They moved to Scotland during early May before returning to Worthy Down later in the month. As news of the imminent evacuation from Dunkirk filtered through, the Skuas were given orders to patrol the beaches and fight off any attacking enemy aircraft.

Although designed as a fighter and dive bomber, the Skua was not really intended for dogfights, unlike the Hurricanes and Spitfires. As they did not have the speed of the fighters, in this role they tended to be cumbersome. Initially the Luftwaffe were wary of this new aircraft but after one or two skirmishes, they got to know that they were no match for the Messerschmitt fighter. Consequently, the FAA lost a lot of them around this period with severe losses in pilots. Their appearance did however give encouragement and strength to the troops below as they struggled to board the many craft waiting off-shore. They did at least know that the RAF and FAA were overhead and in this respect the

Stalwart of the Naval squadrons in Hampshire. A Blackburn Skua of No 803 Squadron Fleet Air Arm. (Crown copyright)

name of Worthy Down would go down in history.

In 1917, 480 acres of the old Winchester racecourse were developed into an airfield. Six large aeroplane sheds were erected together with a sizeable hangar and it was first used by the Wireless and Observers School who arrived in August 1918, but with the armistice, the airfield saw very little action.

In 1924 the site was re-activated when No 58 Squadron re-formed there in April with the Vickers Vimy. They were the sole occupants until April 1927 when they were joined by No 7 Squadron with Vickers Virginias. Both types were a new generation of bombers which if the First World War had continued, would have been used against the Germans. As it was they were the mainstay of the newly emerged Bomber Command during the 20s and early 30s and it was in a Vimy that Alcock and Brown first flew the Atlantic in 1919.

No 7 Squadron began re-arming with the Handley Page Heyford in 1935; 'B' flight of No 7 Squadron was renumbered No 102 Squadron and 'A' flight of 58 Squadron became No 215. When the new units had been formed, Nos 58 and 215 moved to Upper Heyford in January 1936 and in August, Nos 7 and 102 left for Finningley, and Worthy Down awaited the arrival of No 49 Squadron from Bircham Newton. This time it was the single-engined Hawker Hind bomber that landed on Worthy Down's lush grass.

The period from 1926 to 1935 saw a gradual build-up at the airfield. Married quarters were erected together with new administration blocks and in September 1936, the airfield was transferred to No 2 Group Bomber Command.

Peacetime flying continued until 1938 when Worthy Down was transferred to Coastal Command as No 17 (T) Group. The bombers left and in their place came the Avro Ansons of Nos 206 and 233 Squadrons, joined later by the Ansons of No 220 Squadron. These were purely attachments at Worthy Down and were not regular squadrons based there. Already the base had been earmarked to become a FAA shore base and the arrival of No 800 Squadron's aircraft from HMS Courageous heralded this phase of its life. The CO, Lt/Cdr B M H Kendall, immediately began to form No 803 Squadron from 'B' flight equipped with six Ospreys and four Nimrods. The Ospreys were soon withdrawn on the arrival of six Skuas and in April 1939, three Rocs were added to the unit.

With the FAA in residence, Worthy Down became HMS Kestrel on 24th May 1939. No 755 Squadron formed at the same time as a

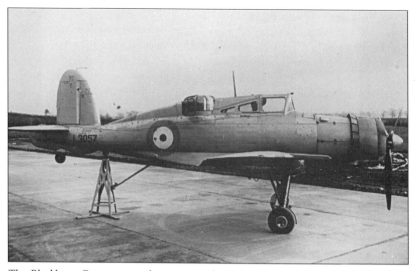

The Blackburn Roc was another type used extensively by the FAA in Hampshire. (MAP)

Telegraphist Air Gunner Training Squadron. It undertook the initial part of the wireless course for TAGs with Blackburn Sharks and a couple of Ospreys. The same date saw No 757 form at Worthy Down, both units forming the No 1 Air Gunners School. Within a few months of the run-up to the war, several other FAA squadrons formed at the airfield and were soon embarked on carriers.

As already seen, Dunkirk proved a busy time for Worthy Down. The Skuas and Rocs did a sterling job over the beaches but were really no match for the enemy aircraft. Though many were lost, some did have some success even to the extent of one Skua shooting down two of the enemy. Incidents like this were however rare.

HMS Kestrel was fully at war by this time and the FAA were at last to get an aircraft that had the same weight of fire-power as the Hurricane and Spitfire yet was to be flown from aircraft carriers. It did not enter regular squadron service until September 1940 and although it was kept a firm secret until then, Worthy Down did have a glimpse of the Fairey Fulmar whilst the Battle of Britain raged overhead. No 808 Squadron formed at the airfield on 1st July 1940 under the command of Lt H E R Torin RN. It received the first of the new fighters for work-up trials proving a 'fine, manoeuvrable aircraft with a good take-off, moderate climb and plenty of endurance'. (Terence Horsley: *Find, Fix*

144

and Strike). Whatever the enemy thought is not recorded, neither is whether or not they knew of this new fighter. It may just be coincidence but Worthy Down was attacked on the 15th August 1940 just as the flying trials of the Fulmar were commencing.

From earlier chapters we have seen that on this particular day many large scale raids were carried out. It came to be known as 'Black Thursday' to the Luftwaffe for despite the large number of aircraft they sent over the UK, the day proved to be the most violent and costly of the entire battle. From early morning the enemy had sent in waves of bombers and fighters, the main targets being the airfields in Kent, Sussex, Surrey and Hampshire. It was in the evening that two major attacks involving some 250 aircraft took place. Junkers 88s of LG 1 operating from Orleans and Bricy were briefed to attack Middle Wallop. Having done so the II Gruppe spotted Worthy Down and turned to attack.

Seeing the enemy was for the naval personnel at Worthy Down something of a novelty as the Luftwaffe had never taken any notice of the base previously. What they did recognise in plenty of time to make for cover was the Balkan cross and the swastika as the JU 88s bore down on them. Falling over themselves to take cover, the ratings and WRNS made it to the shelters as the first bombs were dropped. With a noise like thunder they exploded harmlessly on open grass as the other aircraft came in to drop their load. These too landed on open land and caused very little damage to buildings or aircraft except for the pieces of shrapnel that embedded themselves in both. As the Junkers turned for home they were met head on by the Hurricanes of 43 and 601 Squadrons from Tangmere and the Spitfires of 234 Squadron from nearby Middle Wallop. The enemy suffered grievously, losing eight aircraft in as many minutes. The remainder limped home across the Channel, some not making it and falling into the sea. The loss to the Luftwaffe was 72 aircraft. Later in the day, Goering was to issue an instruction stating that no more than one officer was to be present in any bomber. This was to reduce the officer casualties on bombers which were seriously weakening the strength of his Luftwaffe.

Back at Worthy Down only one hangar had been hit and was repairable. The airfield had escaped lightly but it was noticed that German radio sometime after the attack announced that HMS Kestrel had been sunk!

The 15th August raid was in fact the only time that the airfield was attacked; although enemy aircraft flew overhead constantly, no further

A Seamew I FN628 of No 755 Squadron, Worthy Down. (FAA Museum)

bombing took place. Perhaps this was just as well for with the constant attacks on the Supermarine factory at Eastleigh (Southampton Airport), the dispersal of certain facets of the Spitfire operation became necessary. With the availability of two Bellman hangars at Worthy Down, Spitfire development test flying immediately located there.

Before this, No 808 Squadron had embarked their Fulmars on *HMS Pegasus* having themselves spent a good time in further developing the potential of the aircraft at Worthy Down. The arrival of the test flying facility for Spitfires ensured the future activity of the airfield and in response to the attack on the 15th August, a decoy airfield was laid out at Micheldever. Worthy Down itself was subjected to a 'defence onslaught' when a ring of 32 pill boxes was erected together with a multitude of fire trenches. Whilst the majority of the pill boxes were of the standard 'Type 22', at least two of the 'good idea but useless' Pickett-Hamilton Retractable Gun Forts were placed alongside the landing area. Designed to be raised from ground level in the event of an enemy paratrooper attack, they contained two poor airmen usually armed with Bren guns or rifles who would fire at the enemy through slits in the side of the concrete. When the attack was over, the fort could then be sunk to ground level thus hopefully concealing the entire construction. They fell out of use after 1942 but were never removed.

In 1941, a large aircraft storage park was constructed on the west side of the A34 road. Forty-eight Dutch barns, two Bessoneaux and a Blister hangar offered good cover for the aircraft. This facility combined with the Spitfire test flying and the TGA School kept Worthy Down a very busy airfield.

On 1st December 1942, No 755 Squadron took on the Proctors of No 756 Squadron and the Lysanders of No 757 Squadron when the latter two units disbanded. When the TAG School moved to Canada in 1943, it ended a long association between the air-gunners and the airfield. With Lt/Cdr J J Dykes RNVR assuming command of 755 Squadron, it re-equipped with the Curtiss Seamew. About 250 Seamews were delivered to Britain under the Lend/Lease arrangements. Although intended for catapult launching from warships, the Seamew actually saw no operational service and from 1943 onwards was relegated to a training role. It was not a popular aircraft by any means due to its difficult ground handling and landing characteristics but Worthy Down was to make good use of the aircraft in the training role.

Supermarine test flying continued until March 1944 when it transferred to High Point. The airfield continued to be used by aircraft in distress, the largest one to land being a Liberator but with the forthcoming invasion of France, Worthy Down was used by many different types of aircraft connected with the landings. Prior to this, one of the more unusual squadrons to use the airfield was No 739, a blind approach development unit. With the rapid development of radar, new ways of landing an aircraft in poor visibility were constantly being sought. Equipped with Swordfish, Fulmars, Oxfords and Ansons, 739 arrived in September 1943 staying until 5th October 1944.

One week before the D-Day landings and in common with every other airfield, a security cordon was thrown around Worthy Down. Whilst the airfield did not play a prominent part in the invasion, many troops and stores were based there during the build-up. Such was this influx of men and machines that a spur line was built to connect the base and beyond with the main London and South Western railway line at Alton. Eventually over 16,000 military trains were to use this extension.

From the end of the war until 1947, the base was used to store aircraft awaiting dispersal. With peace came the inevitable economies, including HMS Kestrel, which was paid off in November 1947 and went onto a care and maintenance basis. In the 1960s, the hangars were demolished together with various other buildings. Despite this, parts of the airfield still survive for the intrepid enthusiast to find today.

16
THE REMAINING
AIRFIELDS

Marwell Hall

As established in the chapter on Eastleigh/Southampton airport, the manufacturing company of Cuncliffe-Owen converted several Spitfires into Seafires during 1941. With the conversion work being carried out at Eastleigh, test flying was becoming increasingly difficult from the airfield due to the proliferation of balloon sites around the area. Cuncliffe-Owen's managing director, Mr R Hayes, lived at Marwell Hall, a very large country house surrounded by a lot of ground. It was realised that by removing some hedges and joining several fields together, a sizeable grass strip could be built. The natural wooded area around the house afforded excellent camouflage and with levelling and clearance of debris completed, Marwell Hall opened in 1941. The ferrying of aircraft between Eastleigh and the new field was carried out by the Air Transport Auxiliary who began flying Spitfires and Blenheims into the strip immediately it was open.

By 1942 it was being used by American aircraft the size of Hudsons and Bostons flying in for conversion work. Later in the year Venturas and Liberators landed very warily on the grass strip. The largest aircraft that the ATA ever flew into Marwell Hall was the Halifax and for this aircraft, certain lengthening of the airfield had first to be completed. This entailed building extra hangarage and domestic buildings.

With Marwell Hall working at its peak during late 1943, it was serving its purpose admirably for not only was it a test flight facility for Spitfire production, it also became a major base for modifications and conversions for many types of aircraft. As the German bombing campaign decreased, Cuncliffe-Owen moved back to Eastleigh and Air Service Training took over Marwell Hall to carry out design modifications on Mustangs and Mitchells. With the end of the war its importance became less and by 1946, just the hangars remained, the occupants long gone. Two of the hangars remain today and the hall itself is now the headquarters of the famous zoological park. Though this is a far cry from the major test facility that it was, at least some signs are still visible of its past history.

Hamble

From its humble beginnings as just a landing ground, Hamble grew into a major site for aircraft manufacturing. It is a difficult history for there were three sites bearing the same name, two landbased and one water. The first landing ground known simply as 'Browns' was used by the Admiralty during 1913. During 1914, a site for float-plane manufacture was established beside the River Hamble with a slipway running into the water. Fairey Aviation were the first residents whilst at the land airfield, A V Roe had begun to construct a factory. Completed by 1916, a design team headed by Roy Chadwick, later to achieve great fame with his Lancaster bomber, arrived to begin designing new projects.

On the riverside, work went ahead on building seaplanes but at the coming of the armistice construction stopped although the design team continued to work there. In 1925 all land-plane flying was transferred to a new airfield adjacent to the present one and called Hamble North. Three years later A V Roe sold their interest in the company to Sir W G Armstrong-Whitworth Aircraft Ltd and a new name entered the world of aircraft manufacturing. The company set up a flying school for reserve officers, forming Air Service Training Ltd for the purpose.

With the expansion plans of the RAF and the ominous signs of another war soon, the reserve school became No 3 E & RFTS in April

A scene familiar at many airfields. A Spitfire Mk XII of 91 Squadron at Hamble. (Crown copyright)

1933 retaining the civilian aircraft for this purpose. In the meantime, the old Avro factory on Hamble South airfield, the original site, had also been taken over by Armstrong-Whitworth and had commenced building the civilian Ensign airliner. Production of this aircraft continued until the outbreak of war. In September 1939, the reserve and voluntary training ceased and the No 3 E & RFTS became No 3 EFTS.

Due to its close proximity to the Supermarine works at Eastleigh, No 3 Ferry Pilots Pool of the ATA were based at Hamble during the war to enable the Spitfires to be ferried quickly to the test airfields such as Marwell Hall. An attack by a single Heinkel 111 on the 12th July 1940 prompted the training school to move out and the airfield was left to the manufacturing of aircraft only.

Folland Aircraft Ltd, who had begun building aircraft at Hamble in 1937, were now busy producing component parts for Blenheims and Beauforts and were later to take on sub-contract work on Mosquitos and Wellingtons. The ATA had the job of ferrying all these aircraft to and from their respective airfields throughout the war, the majority of them being flown by female pilots.

Like a few of the airfields in the county, Hamble had a quiet war but played a very important part in the ultimate victory. Conversion work still carried on in peacetime with Folland Aircraft producing the jet powered Midge and later the Gnat at Hamble. The company was absorbed into Hawker Siddeley in 1959 and today is part of British Aerospace producing sub-assemblies for Harriers and Hawks. On the flying side, the RAF established a flying school at Hamble followed by

The College of Air Training at Hamble as it appeared in 1977. Civilian Bulldogs await their trainees. (Portsmouth Publishing)

a similar school for British Airways. Both of them had left by 1979 and flying ceased when the airfield was sold to a developer.

Beaulieu

The most active of the four airfields that were established within the New Forest was most certainly Beaulieu. A First World War site had been built at East Boldre but this was not the same place as that chosen for the second conflict. Originally Beaulieu was intended to be one of the ALGs planned for Hampshire but as building of the site commenced, new plans ensured that it quickly developed into something very much bigger.

In December 1942, the Air Ministry published a schedule of airfield requirements for the immediate future and included in them was a

Many towns throughout the country held Wings for Victory weeks. Most of them were centered around a retired aircraft such as this Vickers Wellington Mk Ic, seen here on its way to Winchester aboard a Queen Mary trailer manufactured by Taskers of Andover. (Hampshire Record Office)

requirement for several VHB (very heavy bomber) airfields. Several sites already built including Beaulieu were chosen with upgrading taking place immediately to bring them up to a standard far in excess of the normal ALG. Beaulieu was one of the first to receive such treatment which upon completion, enabled it to receive a squadron of heavy bombers.

No 224 Squadron had converted to the Consolidated Liberator III at Tiree in July 1942. The Liberator, a large American manufactured four-engined bomber, had started patrols with Coastal Command in the late summer of 1941 and on its first Atlantic patrol in October it went into combat with the enemy. The new aircraft greatly increased the range of patrol which could now stretch out over the Atlantic. With Beaulieu ready, the squadron arrived on 9th September 1942 to begin new operations that included anti-submarine sorties over the Bay of Biscay and attacks on enemy shipping off the French coast.

The airfield came under the wing of Coastal Command and with increased enemy activity around the Bay, No 224 were joined on the 25th October by No 405 (Vancouver) Squadron of the RCAF flying Handley Page Halifax IIs and a few weeks later by similar aircraft of a detachment of No 158 Squadron. This formidable line-up of aircraft was soon achieving success in attacking and sinking the U-boats that were prowling around the Bay of Biscay. The hunting of these submarines was monotonous, grey work but not without its dangers and an account from one of the pilots of a Liberator of 224 Squadron shows how dangerous.

'We dived low and dropped our depth-charges which hit the water very close to the U-boat with an amazing splash. Suddenly the boat began to fire her gun at us with deadly accuracy as I could hear the shells hitting our fuselage. Seconds later the sea erupted all around the submarine as our charges exploded but the shock wave also caught our aircraft and threw us around the sky. Looking back we could see the U-boat was beginning to dive and we think hopefully our attack had left it with weak plates which could give in under a lot of water pressure. For us, it was a long, slow and nerve-racking flight back to base.'

To assist the aircraft to remain airborne longer, the squadrons refuelled at St Eval on the Cornish coast saving them both time and fuel. Later a Czech squadron, No 311 arrived to join the Liberators which allowed the Halifax bombers of No 405 to return to Bomber Command and Topcliffe. No 224 remained until the 23rd April 1943 when they left to be based permanently at St Eval.

The Czech squadron proved themselves masters at stalking and attacking the U-boats. The Luftwaffe equivalent of the Liberator was the Focke-Wulf Condor which the enemy would use in liaison with the U-boat crews. With their natural hatred for an enemy that had taken over their homeland, the Czechs made sure that the Condor was no match for their Liberators. Many were shot down by 311 Squadron aircraft and many U-boats were sent to the bottom of the sea by their depth-charges.

On the 25th September 1943, they were joined by No 53 Squadron again with Liberators. Together the squadrons roamed over large areas of sea catching the U-boats on the surface recharging their batteries. By late 1943 and early 1944 the task was becoming harder as more Schnorkel equipped submarines began to replace the older boats. This new invention allowed the U-boats to remain submerged whilst charging their batteries thus it had to be a very sharp observer to spot a pipe protruding from the ocean surface. After two conversions to more powerful marks of Liberator at Beaulieu, the Czechs left for Predannack on 23rd February 1944.

Before they left and with a change to Fighter Command, No 257 (Burma) Squadron brought their Hawker Typhoon IBs in from Warmwell. Attached to the 2nd TAF, the squadron began fighter/bomber sorties over occupied Europe in softening-up operations before D-Day. They barely stayed a month before moving on to Tangmere. More Typhoons had arrived on the 23rd January 1944 with No 263 (Fellowship of the Bellows) Argentina Squadron who were to be the last RAF unit to use Beaulieu. They moved to Warmwell two weeks later just before the P47 Thunderbolts of the American 365th Fighter Group arrived at the base. This unit operated from the first light of dawn to the last ray of sun in an effort to wear down the enemy before the Allied invasion in June 1944. Further American squadrons used the base, the aircraft acting as escorts and dive-bombers right up to D-Day. One week after the invasion, they had gone. Peace came to this particular airfield for a little while but with its return to the RAF in September 1944, the Airborne Forces Experimental Establishment moved in.

The experiments involved many differing types of aircraft which could be used in support of airborne troops. By 1950 the unit had been absorbed by Boscombe Down and Beaulieu was placed under care and maintenance until 1953. It was then handed back to the USAAF as a reserve base, but with no use by them at all the airfield was derequisitioned and returned to the Forestry Commission in November 1959. Very little remains to be seen today.

Ibsley

Opened in February 1941 as a satellite of Middle Wallop, No 32 Squadron brought their Hurricanes over from the parent station before the site was completed. German reconnaissance aircraft had noted that a new airfield was under construction and promptly attacked Ibsley, dropping over 30 bombs. Despite the added work, No 118 Squadron brought their Spitfire IIAs in on the 18th April 1941 to begin convoy patrols over the Channel as No 32 departed to Pembrey.

The squadron achieved modest success on anti-shipping patrols and when No 234 (Madras Presidency) Squadron arrived at Ibsley on the 5th November 1941 with Spitfires, the two units were able to form a wing. Escort duties were very much in demand and with the addition of No 66 Squadron in April 1942, the airfield became almost a front-line fighter base. As with Beaulieu, Ibsley was handed over to the Americans and the 1st Fighter Group of the 8th Air Force flying the very heavy P38 Lockheed Lightning. The 94th Fighter Squadron, part of the group, flew the first air defence sorties from Ibsley on the 29th August 1942 and the group's first offensive mission was flown on 25th September. Despite success, the fighter group was transferred from the 8th to the 12th Fighter Group eight weeks later as the Lightnings left for operations in Africa after flying 270 sorties from Ibsley.

Nos 66 and 118 Squadrons returned and were later joined by No 504 (County of Nottingham), No 129 (Mysore) and No 616 (South Yorkshire) Squadrons. Once again an all Spitfire wing, they carried out escort operations including American bombers on daylight raids.

In September 1943 three Czech squadrons, Nos 310, 312 and 313 arrived and together with the forementioned units, they alternated between Ibsley and some of the other 11 Group airfields.

The Spitfires gave way to Typhoons when No 263 (Fellowship of the Bellows) Argentina Squadron flew in but by early 1944 the RAF had left Ibsley and the airfield was given over to the Americans. Between April and July 1944, the 367th Fighter Group, flying P38 Lightnings again, carried out close escort work but with the rapid advance of the allied troops in France, their stay was all too short. When they left, Ibsley returned to the RAF but was only used on occasions by some Airspeed Oxfords, a number of Dakotas and finally by No 49 Maintenance Unit. It had become totally inactive by 1947 and was finally derequisitioned.

Holmsley South

Operation 'Torch', the invasion of French North Africa in October 1942, gave birth to the third New Forest airfield, Holmsley South. Constructed over the winter of 1941/42, it was built to provide accommodation for the reinforcements needed to carry out 'Torch'.

RAF personnel arrived long before the airfield was ready followed by eight American Air Force Liberators to commence anti-submarine patrols. No 547 Squadron was formed at Holmsley South in October 1942 as a unit of Coastal Command with Vickers Wellington VIIIs. It began training as an anti-submarine squadron but was also adept at bombing and torpedo dropping. When 'Torch' was completed, the American Liberators returned to Alconbury and 547 moved on to Chivenor. On the 2nd December 1942 No 58 flew in with Halifax bombers and in the new year they were joined by No 502 (Ulster) also flying the Halifax. This was not really the ideal aircraft for anti-submarine work and the squadrons suffered considerable losses, returning to Bomber Command in early 1944.

Holmsley reverted to No 10 Group of Fighter Command and became home to three Canadian squadrons, 441 (Silver Fox), 442 (Caribou) and 443 (Hornet), all of them arriving on the 18th March equipped with Spitfires. Together they formed No 144 Wing and were later joined by another wing, No 121 with Typhoons and comprising Nos 174 (Mauritius), 175 and 245 (Northern Rhodesia) Squadrons. Holmsley was becoming very busy indeed! No 121 Wing specialised in support work with the army on the ground and their rocket firing Typhoons certainly ensured a smoother path for the infantry troops. A further Canadian squadron, No 418 (City of Edmonton) also arrived at Holmsley on 8th April 1944 flying the Mosquito II. As with all the other New Forest airfields and ALGs the period of intense activity did not last long, the time being dictated by the demands and progress of the invading allied troops. Thus No 121 moved to France on 20th June 1944 to be replaced by three Mustang squadrons, Nos 129 (Mysore), 306 (Torun) Polish Squadron and 315 (Deblin), another Polish unit. Whilst the Mustang was a good close support aircraft, it was no fighter and considerable losses were incurred at the hands of the Luftwaffe, still very active even at this late stage of the war. They stayed for five days before departing to Ford and in common with the rest of the Forest airfields, Holmsley South became home to the Americans.

This time it was a bomber group, the 349th. Three squadrons, Nos 584, 585 and 587 of the USAAF's IXth Air Force flew in from Boreham flying B26 Marauders to carry out medium level bombing attacks behind enemy lines in France; it was once again a short visit, the airfield returning to the RAF in October 1944. Transport Command used Holmsley for flying liberation trips to the Continent and No 246 Squadron commenced service flights to the Middle and Far East. In

1946, a Battle of Britain RAF At Home display was held, this being the last major event at Holmsley South. One month later the field was under Care and Maintenance and slowly returned to the Forestry Commission.

Stoney Cross

Intended as one of the ALGs for Hampshire, the decision was taken in 1942 to develop the site for extensive fighter operations. Mustangs of Nos 26 and 175 squadrons arrived for a brief stay but with the airfield nowhere near completion, no units used the base for several months.

June 1943 saw Stoney Cross transferred to No 10 Group with No 297 Squadron bringing their Whitleys and Albemarles in together with a number of American B17 Flying Fortresses. This was a temporary situation with a permanent squadron arriving one year later. The first unit was 'B' Flight of 297 Squadron which was renumbered 299 and reformed at Stoney Cross on the 4th November 1943 equipped with the American Lockheed Ventura, a type of super Hudson. These were replaced by the Short Stirling IV in January 1944 whereupon training began with the airborne forces. No 299 were joined by 'A' Flight of No 297 in September 1943, they in turn taking over the Albemarles of the parent squadron.

March 1944 saw the Americans arrive as Stoney Cross went the same way as the other Forest sites. Nos 397, 393 and 394 Squadrons of the USAAF arrived with Lightnings and immediately began an intensive training schedule in support of D-Day. Further American units used the airfield for very brief periods until D-Day when the airfield returned to the RAF.

No 1 Heavy Glider Servicing Unit moved in together with a reformed 232 Squadron with six Wellingtons. Many various types of bombers and fighters passed through the airfield until 1946 when it went to Care and Maintenance before being finally derequisitioned in January 1948 and returned to the Forestry Commission.

17
THE ADVANCED
LANDING GROUNDS

With the Battle of Britain over and the war being carried to the enemy during 1941 and 1942, thoughts were turning to an allied invasion of the French coast. It was obvious that such a task would require a tremendous air effort and that many new airfields would be required. Because there was so little time to construct permanent sites it was decided that airstrips incorporating the basic facilities would have to suffice. The proposed airstrips were to be called Advanced Landing Grounds (ALGs), comprising Sommerfeld Track runways, refuelling and re-arming sites, hard perimeter tracks and blister hangars. Accommodation would be tented with just a few huts for essential personnel.

During 1942 a number of surveys were carried out at potential sites in the south east of England. Seventy-two possible sites were surveyed with the planned completion date of March 1943. Ideally the main runway was to be 4,800 ft in length with a secondary runway of 4,200 ft. Construction of the sites would be given to the Royal Engineer Construction Groups and the RAF Construction Groups with help later coming from the American Engineer Aviation Battalions to enable a quicker result if required. By the time the 72 sites had been surveyed, the number had been whittled down to 32 and still later to 25.

Most of the chosen sites met with fierce opposition from the local landowners who feared the land would never be returned to them. They also objected to the felling of trees, the filling of dykes and ditches and the removal of hedges, all of which were necessary to ensure safety for flying operations.

Sommerfeld tracking was laid at most of the ALGs to give better landings and take-offs. Unfortunately it also damaged aircraft tyres and undercarriages.

Working on grading and clearing began immediately after the 25 sites selected had been approved. Despite good progress by the construction gangs, the bad winter of 1942/43 plus the shortage of certain materials caused a fairly drastic delay in completion. This put back the final date for use to the summer of 1943. Once again the number of ALGs required was revised and reduced to 23 and although two were designed for light bomber use, they all became fighter airstrips.

All-weather serviceability was provided by laying Sommerfeld Track on the grass. This was a rigid and heavy steel netting held in place by pickets. Designed by an Austrian, Kurt Sommerfeld, it had been in production since 1941 and whilst the initial trials had proved successful, large aircraft such as the American Thunderbolt were inclined to tear it up when landing a little heavily. From 1943 onwards, the British Reinforced Engineering Co Ltd developed another type of mesh mat, Square Mesh Track, and this was readily available as a replacement for Sommerfeld Track during the spring of 1944.

Despite all the problems and setbacks, the ALGs were ready for use by 1st April 1944, just in time for 'Operation Overlord', the allied invasion of Europe which took place on 6th June 1944 and known as 'D-Day'. Hampshire was to receive five ALGs of a significant size, all of them seeing heavy usage. The one thing that they had in common with all the other sites in the south-east was that they were intended to be used for a few months only, the time depending on the success of the allied landings. They were all to be sited within a few miles of the Channel coast and as such were grouped in four main areas. Ashford and New Romney in Kent, Chichester in Sussex and the New Forest area in Hampshire.

Bisterne

Situated $1\frac{1}{2}$ miles south of Ringwood, and now in Dorset, Bisterne was surveyed in the original batch in 1942 and was completed in September 1943. Although it received the basic facilities, it also had many extras such as taxiways and hard-standings constructed in tarmac. After completion it remained dormant until the 10th April 1944 when the 371st Fighter Group of the 9th Tactical Air Force arrived with their P47 Thunderbolts. This was a very heavy fighter of enormous size and after a number of heavy landings, the Sommerfeld Track began to tear. The Fighter Group moved over to nearby Ibsley to enable repairs to be carried out. Upon their return to Bisterne, the group flew daily in support of the D-Day landings. On the 6th June they flew dive-bombing missions ahead of the landing troops and continued these operations until the unit moved to France in July 1944. No further use was made of Bisterne and the ALG returned to agriculture during 1945, the Sommerfeld Track being lifted and sold for scrap. Very few signs remain today.

Frost Hill Farm

This ALG went into the history books as being one of the sites ready for use during the Battle of Britain. Although then just a series of large grass landing areas, it was once again surveyed for upgrading to ALG status during June 1942. In June 1940 the site was classified as a scatter or emergency landing ground for Odiham. It was covered in easily removable poles to prevent enemy aircraft landing during this time but there is no record of the site being used by Odiham-based aircraft. Work went ahead in 1942 on constructing the ALG with two Sommerfeld Track runways being laid during 1943. Curiously no buildings or blister hangars were erected, an indication perhaps that by the time the track had been laid, the ALG had already been recognised as too far away from the coast or even just unsuitable. Frost Hill Farm was never used in anger yet today it finds use as a landing ground for helicopters of the Army Air Corps from nearby Middle Wallop. The Sommerfeld Track was removed in 1945 but occasional pieces are still being unearthed today. It is the only remaining ALG still in use in the county.

Larks Barrow

Situated $1\frac{1}{2}$ miles north west of Whitchurch, this site was surveyed in June 1942 as a second line ALG. It proved a difficult task to construct due to the amount of tree-felling required and the heavy grading work. It was proposed to build two 4,500 ft runways but at the beginning of 1943, the Air Ministry decided that Larks Barrow was surplus to requirements. Despite the amount of work already done on the ALG, it never became active and was only used as a relief landing ground for local airfields. No Sommerfeld Track was ever laid thus making the site an easy task to return to agriculture, which it did in 1945. No signs of the ALG remain today.

Lymington

In direct contrast to the last two sites, Lymington saw considerable use. Situated at Snooks Farm, about a mile east of Lymington, it was also

No 257 Squadron at Needs Ore Point just before D-Day

known as Pylewell. Surveyed in 1942, it became a priority site with two temporary runways being laid with Sommerfeld Track. Several blister hangars were erected together with limited maintenance facilities. During March 1944, the American 50th Fighter Group from the 9th TAF moved in. Comprising Nos 10, 81 and 313 Squadrons, all flying the P47 Thunderbolt, they carried out their first mission on 1st May 1944 when they attacked communication targets in Northern France. These attacks continued up to and after D-Day, the group finally leaving for the Continent in the middle of June. The site was soon derequisitioned and returned to agriculture, one of the blister hangars remaining to this day for the storage of agricultural equipment.

Needs Ore Point

One of the most active sites, Needs Ore Point was surveyed in 1942 and was established as an ALG by the middle of 1943. Built on fairly flat ground to the west of the entrance to the Beaulieu river in the New Forest, it was completed in time to enable Nos 257 (Burma), 266 (Rhodesia) and 197 Squadrons to bring their Typhoon IBs in from Tangmere. Employed on attacking enemy transport and troop concentrations on the Continent, the aircraft were equipped with 500 lb bombs. They were joined the next day by No 193 (Fellowship of the Bellows) Squadron from Llanbedr also with Typhoons. This brought the total number of Typhoons at Needs Ore Point to 150. From a relatively quiet existence, the ALG suddenly became one of the noisiest places in the county. Needs Ore Point was stretched to capacity as the aircrews were further strengthened and supported by 900 men and 200 lorries. It was estimated that there was a take-off and landing every 45 seconds as the run-up to D-Day began. So intensive was the activity that it is said no other airfield in the UK could boast of such a hectic period. By July 1944 silence had returned and Needs Ore Point became surplus to requirements. It did not die as suddenly as the others for the Royal Navy used it for storage purposes until 1946 when it was derequisitioned and returned to agriculture.

Winkton

The third of the New Forest ALGs was also known as Sopley though this is not to be confused with the location of the GCI (Ground Controlled Interception) set up for the control of night-fighters around 1941. Ready by September 1943, it was not used until April 1944. Once again it was the Americans who used Winkton when the 404th Fighter Group consisting of Nos 506, 507 and 508 Squadrons arrived. Their P.47 Thunderbolts operated as fighter/bombers and were tasked with destroying V1 sites in France. On D Day they provided top cover for the landing troops and flew a total of 191 missions from Winkton. When they left for France on 19th June 1944, no further use was made of the ALG and like all the other sites, it returned to agriculture.

18
CIVILIANS
AT WAR

Although generally regarded as a reserve area by the military in 1938/
39, Hampshire and its civilian population certainly saw war and its
effects at first hand. With the close proximity of the large naval base at
Portsmouth and the Supermarine aircraft factory at Southampton, it
soon became obvious that the county would be a target for the enemy.
The War Office, Admiralty and Air Ministry did not consider
Hampshire a front line county such as Kent, Surrey and Sussex but
the civilian authorities and the public alike did not agree. As with the
rest of the country, the civilian organisations became essential to the
war effort at home and were managed by the local authority which
came under the control of the Ministry of Home Security, Hampshire
being No 6 (Southern) Region with its headquarters at Reading in
Berkshire.

The expected bombing gave birth to a number of civilian rescue and
welfare services. To cope with the aftermath of bombing and to
forewarn civilians of an impending raid was the responsibility of the
Air Raid Precautions services (ARP). First introduced in 1935 when the
rumblings of a war with Germany were first heard, it was a mainly
volunteer organisation, the members being able to retain their full-time
occupations. They had to report exactly where the bombs fell and be
able to guide the rescue, medical and mortuary services to the incident.
In addition they were responsible for the civilian air-raid shelters and
to ensure that not a chink of light showed through the black-out
curtains of the houses at night. Indeed one of the more familiar calls

associated with the ARP was 'put that light out', a saying that became the ridicule of the organisation and the butt of many cartoonists' jokes. Whilst the ARP wardens did not fight the many fires that enemy bombing caused, they did assist the fire-brigades and ambulance personnel in locating disaster areas.

From 1938 onwards, the local fire-brigades had the task of fighting the fires assisted by the Auxiliary Fire Service (AFS), another part-time organisation. The auxiliaries did a sterling job during the Battle of Britain and when they eventually became part of the National Fire Service during 1941, a friendly rivalry sprang up between the former auxiliaries and the regular firemen.

In September 1941, once again the voluntary organisations came under one umbrella, that of the Civil Defence. An essentially passive organisation, the role was to mitigate the effects of enemy attack. By this time, Civil Defence was on a more controlled basis and instruction was continually given to learn and co-ordinate measures against attack.

Before the outbreak of war, the press, both local and international, had conditioned the civilian population on what to expect when war came. Articles spoke of gas attacks and devastating air-raids within hours of war being announced. In order that the county be prepared for such eventualities, gas masks were issued to every man, woman and child. Not everyone however heeded the advice to carry them everywhere and with the 'phoney war' occurring just after the declaration of war, even fewer people were seen with them over their shoulders!

Before all of these preparations, the air-raid system was regularly tested. Sirens were set up at strategic points in the county and both the 'air raid imminent' and 'all clear' sounds were regularly heard. At first the sound was frightening to some people but as time progressed, the populace eventually got used to it and at the first tones of the 'raid imminent', made for the shelters.

Then there was the security. A cordon was put around every airfield and civilians having to pass through the area were issued with passes which had to be shown to the guards. In the case of Eastleigh (Southampton) airfield, the home of the Supermarine test facility, the security was in the hands of the Hampshire Regiment, as Mrs Elliot of Eastleigh, whose husband served in the regiment, recalls:

'Living about a half mile from the airport, I got used to the sound of aircraft. I remember that the field was then called HMS Raven and to get to the guard-room you had to cross the main railway line and go

King George VI and Queen Elizabeth visiting a Canadian infantry division at Aldershot. Many men and women from the Empire came to help the defence of Britain. (Hampshire Record Office)

under a small bridge. I was working for the railway at the time. Opposite the guard-room was a small lane where there was a pill-box with Bofors guns. I remember that later in the war the Germans dropped two landmines close by killing all the lads manning it. I actually met my husband at Eastleigh and luckily we both survived the war'.

Apart from the obvious dangers of war, the residents of Hampshire also had to put up with food rationing. Initially it was just butter, sugar and bacon that required coupons, with meat following in March 1940. The limitations on the British 'cuppa' seemed to have the worst effect with two ounces of tea per person per week being the norm. Later the rationing spread to cheese, eggs, milk, bread and finally to canned foods. People were encouraged to dig up their lawns and plant vegetables in order to supplement these meagre rations and the practice of owning an allotment began to flourish.

Food however was not the only restriction on everyday living. In

June 1941, clothes and textiles were rationed with examples such as a man's cotton vest that cost 2s 3d would require four coupons and a lady's bra costing 2s 9½d would only need one coupon. It appeared that the fairer sex needed more underclothes than a man. As the austerity of war began to bite and much to the delight of many small boys, soap was subject to rationing although a good scrubbing brush was not, and without soap, small boys were scrubbed for several moments longer!

Throughout all this hardship however, the civilian population still had time for a smile and the rationing did much to bring everybody to the same level. No more was the attitude 'them and us' prevalent for all classes pulled together for the common good and the chance to beat the enemy.

Another very important aspect of the period was the evacuation of children from built-up and potentially dangerous areas. As early as August 1939, plans had been drawn up for this procedure. The national and local authorities feared that the east coast and the home counties including London would be most at risk with every city in the country eventually being destroyed by bombs and the population gassed. It was therefore decided to evacuate the cities and large towns of all people except those needed to run offices and factories. In the end it was the children that received priority and although still officially on summer holidays, 748,883 children said goodbye to their parents in 1939, and reported to the schools where they were registered. Some reception areas allocated children to specific families while others were deposited in big halls until taken by a family. All the children carried a label attached to their jacket lapel indicating their name, address and religion. Gas-masks and a small case of clothes were usually carried together with one personal item, perhaps a favourite Teddy bear. Life for the evacuees was not always good. Whereas the majority of families welcomed the children into their homes with love and affection, a few were exploited with the householder keeping the allowance and feeding the evacuee with as little as possible. In due course, parents were able to visit their children and because no bombing had taken place straight away, some returned home to take their chances. Later on the blitz drove them out of the cities again and even during the V1 and V2 rocket attacks, more children than ever were evacuated. Hampshire was generally regarded as a reception area but with Portsmouth and Southampton being considered potential targets, children from these towns were evacuated from Hampshire to the Midlands and the West Country.

For many of the children from the large cities, just going to the countryside was itself an eduation. Those of school age still had to go to school but the prospect of helping on a farm or going fruit picking when school closed was ample compensation. For many of the older children, it was their first taste of independence.

For adults left behind who for some reason had been denied a place in the services, there was always the Observer Corps or the Local Defence Volunteers for the men and munitions work or Land Army for the women. The Observer Corps has been covered in an earlier chapter but it was the threat of an invasion that gave birth to a part-time militia. With the evacuation of the BEF from Dunkirk complete, May 1940 saw recruitment begin for men between the ages of 17 and 65 who did not already have a part-time duty in the Civil Defence. Anthony Eden, the new Secretary of State for War, broadcast a radio appeal on the 14th May for men to join a new force to be called the Local Defence Volunteers. Such was the response that by July, the number of recruits had increased to a million and a half. They were renamed the Home Guard in July and the LDV armbands gave way to fatigue battledress and later to normal army uniform. They were instantly nicknamed 'Dad's Army' but were as willing and as intent as anyone in the services. It was not all a case of 'don't panic'.

As an island, Britain needed to be as self-sufficient as possible and immediately war was declared at 11 am on Sunday 3rd September, a follow-up radio announcement stated that the War Agriculture Committee had the authority to requisition all possible land that was capable of being ploughed. This presented a problem to some farmers who did not have the equipment to plough up fields. In these cases the committee came to their aid by allowing farmers to hire equipment from the Ministry at preferential rates. Large areas of heathland were ploughed up including the Wiltshire and Sussex Downs. These of course had to be planted with crops and by the autumn it had to be harvested. Many of the young men who were previously farm workers were now in the services and the shortfall was made up by the Women's Land Army. Eventually over 17,000 young women were employed working from dawn to dusk. The national average wage of £4 paid to them was sometimes supplemented by the farmer allowing them to stay with his own family or letting them have a cottage on the farm. Others stayed in houses or hostels in the nearest village but whatever accommodation was provided, the work proved physically demanding to all the girls, but without their efforts the shortage of food

A Heinkel HE111 of KG55 which fell to the guns of Hurricanes of No 43 Squadron. It crash-landed opposite the Horse and Jockey Inn at Hipley at 4.24 pm on 12th July 1940. One of the crew died in the crash the other three were injured. (Hampshire Record Office)

would have been another problem to contend with.

As with the rest of the country, the bombing had a dramatic effect on the citizens of Hampshire. Just a glance at the incident reports compiled by the local constabulary and the civil defence for 1940 gives an indication of just how much the county suffered.

30.6.40 *Winchester – Micheldever Station.* 11 bombs dropped between station and village. 7 failed to explode, no damage to property.

12.7.40 Enemy plane shot down opposite Horse and Jockey Inn. Crew of Heinkel taken prisoner. 1 dead. Incident took place at Hipley. [The crew were Oblt Kleinhans – killed. Fw Kalina, Ober Fw Knecht and Ober Fw Muller, all wounded. Fw Mohn captured unhurt. Aircraft shot down by 'B' Flight of 43 Squadron].

This Junkers 88 of KG 51 crashed at Horse Pasture farm near Westbourne on Monday 12 August 1940. 3 crewmen perished in the crash with one parachuting to safety. (Portsmouth Publishing)

30.7.40 Unidentified plane crashed behind Woolston – plane on fire. The Chief Constable informed that 2 parachutists had been captured.

1.8.40 Leaflets dropped by enemy aircraft in the region of the New Forest informing Britain that it had already lost the war.

19.8.40 Worthy Down Aerodrome – 4 bombs dropped, 3 on airfield, 1 alongside. Time 1600 hrs.

29.8.40 Enemy aircraft, HE 111 crashed at Hale. 4 crew, 2 wounded and considerable damage done to property. [Aircraft belong to Luftflotte 3, KG 27. Heinkel 111 (3438) shot down by P/O Wright of No 92 Squadron during night operations. Crashed at Hale 2300 hrs. Oblt Huenerbein, Uffz Schlosser, Uffz Sieberd and Ober Gefr Walpert all baled out and were captured. Walpert later died of his injuries].

9.9.40 Petersfield – enemy fighter crashed in flames at Sundown Farm, Ditcham. Aircraft burnt out and pilot killed.

Another angle on the same JU 88 of KG 51. (Portsmouth Publishing)

[Aircraft ME 109E 6139, belonged to JG 53 and crashed at 1815 hrs. Gefr Becker killed].
The Hants Control Incident Chart states bombs falling on the county every day during 1940.
8.10.40 JU 88 flew over Eastleigh bombing and machine gunning. Some bombs fell onto aerodrome sheds. 2 men killed, 2 men and 1 Wren seriously hurt, 12 men and women slightly injured.

These few incidents are indicative of everyday life from May 1940 until virtually the end of the war in Hampshire. Although the county had suffered sporadic attacks during the spring of 1940, the Battle of Britain saw the commencement of the real onslaught. On Saturday 24th August came one of the worst raids on Portsmouth. It was an afternoon attack and involved about 100 aircraft, both bombers and fighters of Luftflotte 3. With the sector station at Middle Wallop also under fire, the force was not detected until they were approaching the coast. Just one fighter squadron was near enough to intercept and the enemy had much of the sky to themselves. The 50 bombers over the city of Portsmouth were heavily attacked by the anti-aircraft guns and

In the last big raid of 1940 on Portsmouth, Christmas Eve saw 13 people killed when the Conway Street area was hit. The salvaging of personal belongings began on Christmas Day. (Portsmouth Publishing)

dropped their bombs haphazardly over the town as well as the dockyard. To one man who was employed as an electrician in the yard, the full horror of war was suddenly staring him in the face. Mr Laurie Upton, now a very youthful 80 plus, recalls the terrible daylight raid.

'I remember it was early afternoon on the 24th when this particular raid took place. Some 50 bombers came over and dropped 60 odd high explosive bombs on Portsmouth centre, not counting those dropped on the dockyard. One particular bomb penetrated the iron ventilating grille of an underground shelter which was actually one of the vaults which ran under the blockmills and were once used for prisoners of war from the Napoleonic period. From 1939 onwards, these vaults had been used for storing large barrels of non-ferrous metal pieces collected from the various machine shops. The bomb came through the grille and exploded underground blowing the pieces of metal from the barrels

The 12th August 1940 attack on Portsmouth dockyard as seen from the nose of a German JU 88. One of the targets is the old WWI battleship HMS Queen Elizabeth, *seen in the foreground. (Via James Moore)*

The disruption to everyday life is all too evident in this photograph of Commercial Road, in the city centre, after a raid. (Portsmouth Publishing)

everywhere. This totally mutilated the dockyard workers sheltering inside. Just along the passage was another vault where the same explosion had sucked all the air out of the shelter together with the air in the lungs of the poor men sitting there. They died without a blemish on their bodies.'

One hundred and seventeen people lost their lives on that one afternoon, many being killed in air-raid shelters. A further 143 suffered terrible injuries, again many of them taking cover in what they presumed were safe places. As it was a Saturday, despite the war people were still determined to enjoy their leisure. Some were caught out in the open for the warning sirens appeared to sound just too late. By then the enemy was overhead. One lady who wishes to remain anonymous was trying to get on with her life.

'On that Saturday it was my sister's birthday and so we planned to celebrate it with a picnic up on Portsdown Hill. Just as we had laid out

174

No smiles on the faces of residents of the Fratton area of Portsmouth when a Tip and Run raid on Sunday 27th October 1940 left them homeless. (Portsmouth Publishing)

the rugs and got the Thermos flasks out, we heard a siren sound in the distance so we hurriedly packed our things and ran down to the nearest shelter. By this time the German aircraft were overhead and the noise was terrible and although we should have gone directly into the shelter, we climbed on to the top and just watched. Can you imagine what this was like, seeing this lovely city being bombed and knowing that your family were in the midst of it all? To make matters worse when the Germans flew over the top of Portsdown Hill they machine-gunned the people caught out in the open. When the all-clear sounded we rushed into the city, luckily to find all our family were safe. So relieved were we that all we could do was laugh and think about the most awful way to spend a birthday tea.'

This and most of the early raids on Portsmouth and the dockyard were all carried out in daylight but from January 1941, the night blitz took over. One of the most feared methods of attack used by the enemy

As Eagle Day approached, the sortie roster for the bombing of Britain was made up. Portsmouth was one of the prime targets on the list. (Plaistow Pictorial)

was the dropping of parachute mines. In all some 38 of the devices were dropped around the area devastating large communities. With so many bombs dropped, the gas, electricity and water supplies were often cut off for many days, bringing further hardship to the civilians. Strangely enough, the dockyard electricity power station was not damaged and eventually was able to supply electricity to the city by being linked into the grid system. One particular incident however did bring a greater sense of danger to the dockyard. A parachute mine landed on one of the 240 ton cranes and remained suspended throughout the night. The following morning volunteer dockyard men, praying that a strong wind would not get up and dislodge it, gently lowered the bomb to the ground. The strange thing was that finding volunteers took longer than the process of lowering the mine and getting the army to defuse it (related by Laurie Upton).

It was not only the dockyard that received all the attention on that fateful Saturday. The Princes Theatre in the city centre was packed with children and their parents during the children's matinée. For a few hours the audience hoped that they could forget about the war and were thus oblivious to the sirens wailing outside. Although a message warning that a raid was imminent was hurriedly displayed on the screen, it was only seconds before the theatre sustained a direct hit by a single bomb. Miraculously, no one was killed although there were many injuries. The sound of the children crying was soon drowned by the noise of the rescue services arriving and immediately work began on removing the rubble and dowsing the fire that had started in the roof timbers. The firemen were quickly followed by the wardens and first-aid parties together with the rescuers, ambulance and salvage departments. Within minutes of the attack they began to bring out the terrified children and their parents. The Baptist church adjoining the theatre, which was another notable building, was also extensively damaged by this same bomb.

The suburbs of this fine city also suffered and there were few streets that escaped the attentions of Nazi raiders. Southsea seemed to attract a lot of bombing with Chelsea Road, Grove Road and St James Road in the city being particularly badly hit. Cosham, Hilsea and Portsea Island itself all suffered material damage.

Portsmouth however was just one of the many Hampshire towns to suffer badly. Most of them had a defence system in the shape of barrage balloons ringed around the outer boundaries. As the enemy became aware of this barrage, a lone fighter would attack the balloons ahead of the main bomber force, shooting down sufficient numbers to make bomb aiming easier. In June 1941, a new type of defence measure came into operation for vulnerable areas such as the dockyard and the Supermarine factory. Manned by the army, it was a mobile smoke generator which proved very effective for it obscured many military targets from the Luftwaffe. This however, was to be at the expense of the surrounding areas unprotected by the smoke screen.

Other inventions were forthcoming in defence of the realm, not all of them very effective. The Hampshire Control Incident Chart now in the county archives gives a strange report for the 10th March 1941.

'A number of cotton parachutes marked 'Littlewoods–Liverpool' were found with 1,200 ft of thin steel wire, some 4" in diameter and some 9". Also some strange rubber parachutes were dropped all over the countryside marked UK'. Strange indeed! Two days later a report read: 'Time unknown, place Chandlers Ford. Mysterious yellow balls found in ditch. After careful examination they were found to be a new type of fungus. Definitely harmful if eaten!' It was little incidents like this that brought a glimmer of humour to a time of terror.

In 1941 the bombing campaign increased against the civilians in

Part of the defence of Portsmouth was entrusted to No 932 Squadron, RAF Balloon Command, seen here at their site among ordinary houses. (Hampshire Record Office)

On the 7th July 1941, Southampton received a raid which killed 26 people. The corner of Northam Road was particularly badly hit. (Southern Newspapers)

Hampshire. Southampton was badly hit on the night of the 6th and 7th of June. Again, on the night of the 7th and 8th of July, in very clear weather, it endured another raid when the Luftwaffe roamed overhead for two hours indiscriminately bombing civilian targets and leaving 26 people dead with many others suffering horrific injuries. There were to be many more similar attacks on the town. Even the Isle of Wight was not spared death and destruction. The Ventnor radar installation was an obvious target. The island had first received bomb attacks in June 1940. These continued through 1941 and 1942 resulting in many deaths and injuries. Freshwater Bay in fact was one of the first towns on the island to endure a new tactic used by the enemy, called Jagdbombenangriff. Since 1940 ME 109s had been fitted with bomb racks but it was not until the 5th March 1942 that they came into real use, when Freshwater Bay was attacked. The bombs killed three elderly people and caused widespread devastation. Cowes had a similar attack on the 28th April but on the night of the 4th/5th May the naval town received its biggest raid to date. It was known as a Baedeker raid.

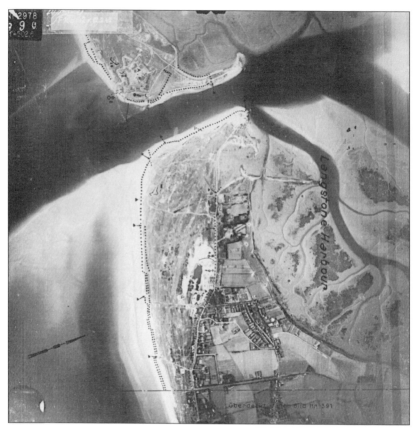

German reconnaissance aircraft were frequently taking new photographs of their intended targets. This is a shot taken by the Luftwaffe on 12 February 1942 of Langstone Harbour with Eastney and Fort Cumberland to the lower left and Sinah Common on Hayling Island in the centre of the photograph. (Plaistow Pictorial)

The name came from a Karl Baedeker, a German publisher of foreign travel guides. It was perhaps appropriate that the Germans should call this particular type of raid 'Baedeker' for the attacks were reprisals against British cities and large towns which contained ancient monuments identified from Baedeker's books. Since April 1942 these reprisal raids had been carried out on cities such as Bath, Norwich and Exeter and large towns such as Southampton, Poole and Grimsby.

One of the Wings for Victory displays at Andover in 1943. Each town competed to see who could raise the most money. On one occasion, Alton raised £253,841; enough to buy six Lancaster bombers for the RAF. (Hampshire Record Office)

For Cowes, the raid began shortly before 11 pm when flares were dropped over the town. A short time later about 50 enemy aircraft came over, some returning later to carry on the attack after refuelling and re-arming back at base. The all-clear was sounded at 3.30 am but the devastation left by over 200 tons of bombs was appalling. Although not a town of great architectural interest, it was assumed that Cowes was on the Baedeker list by virtue of it being a shipyard and the fact that the Polish destroyer *Blyskawica* was undergoing a refit there. Sixty-six people were killed and over 70 injured with the Luftwaffe claiming it as a major attack.

By the end of June and after the frequent Baedeker reprisals, further raids of a similar nature were carried out against smaller and non-cathedral cities and towns. Southampton was to receive another bad raid on the nights of 21st and 22nd June 1942. The total number of significant Baedeker raids was only around 14 but in terms of destruction and loss of life in Britain, it was a holocaust. The raids were replaced by daylight fighter/bomber attacks often with eight or ten aircraft. Once again Hampshire was in the front line as the German tactics were to fly low and therefore undetected by radar before climbing to cross the coast and fly inland to attack the major towns. The ME 109s were supplemented by the faster and more powerful FW 190, both aircraft eventually contributing to the civilian casualty list of 3,236 killed and 4,148 seriously injured and admitted to hospital during 1942.

These figures relate to just one year of a six-year conflict during which the civilian population came face to face with real war. Despite all their efforts, the German military could not dampen the resolve and spirit of the people. Like the majority of the southern counties, Hampshire saw the full horror of war. By 1945 the county had grown tired of it. One of the most distressing physical aspects of civilian life during this period was that night after night life was continually interrupted by sirens, bombs and danger. General Eisenhower observed 'Indignity and inconvenience had been heaped upon the British people almost to breaking point'. How right he was for indirectly it had become a people's as well as a military war and in 1945 when victory was finally achieved, the ultimate acclaim was to come from Winston Churchill in a VE day speech.

'In the long years to come not only will the people of this island but of the world, wherever the bird of freedom chirps in human hearts, look back to what we've done and they will say "Do not despair, do not yield to tyranny, march straight forward and die if need be – unconquered".'

Appendix A

THE SQUADRONS OF THE ROYAL AIR FORCE THAT WERE BASED AT
HAMPSHIRE AIRFIELDS BEFORE, DURING AND AFTER THE SECOND
WORLD WAR

ANDOVER – 2, 9, 11, 12, 13, 16, 21, 44, 53, 59, 63, 81, 82, 101, 103, 104, 105, 106, 107, 116, 119, 142, 148, 169, 170, 207, 214, 215, 225, 285, 289, 296, 613.
BLACKBUSHE – 16, 69, 88, 107, 140, 162, 167, 171, 226, 264, 301, 305, 322, 342, 605, 613, 622.
BEAULIEU – 53, 79, 84, 103, 117, 224, 257, 263, 311.
CHATTIS HILL – 91, 92, 93.
CHILBOLTON – 26, 54, 174, 183, 184, 238, 245, 247, 308, 501, 504.
EASTLEIGH – 7, 28, 42, 45, 224, 266, 269.
FARNBOROUGH – 1, 2, 4, 5, 6, 7, 8, 10, 15, 30, 53, 70, 100, 101, 108.
GOSPORT – 3, 8, 13, 14, 17, 22, 23, 28, 29, 40, 41, 42, 45, 48, 56, 78, 79, 86, 88, 180, 186, 210, 233, 248, 608, 667.
HOLMSLEY SOUTH – 58, 129, 167, 174, 175, 182, 184, 245, 246, 295, 306, 315, 502, 547.
IBSLEY – 32, 66, 118, 124, 129, 165, 234, 263, 268, 310, 312, 313, 501, 504, 616.
LASHAM – 107, 175, 181, 182, 183, 305, 320, 602, 609, 613.
LEE-ON-SOLENT – 26, 33.
MIDDLE WALLOP – 16, 19, 23, 32, 56, 93, 125, 151, 164, 169, 182, 234, 236, 238, 245, 247, 288, 437, 501, 504, 601, 604, 609.
ODIHAM – 2, 4, 13, 18, 26, 33, 46, 53, 54, 59, 63, 66, 72, 96, 130, 168, 170, 171, 174, 175, 182, 184, 225, 230, 233, 247, 264, 268, 271, 604, 613, 614.
STONEY CROSS – 26, 46, 175, 232, 239, 242, 296, 297, 299.
WORTHY DOWN – 7, 35, 49, 58, 102, 207, 215.

Appendix B

THE SQUADRONS OF THE FLEET AIR ARM THAT WERE BASED AT
HAMPSHIRE AIRFIELDS BEFORE, DURING AND AFTER THE SECOND
WORLD WAR

EASTLEIGH – 716, 758, 759, 760, 780, 800, 801, 802, 810, 811, 814, 816, 820, 821,
822, 825, 829.
GOSPORT – 705, 706, 707, 708, 720, 727, 764, 771, 778, 799, 800, 801, 807, 809,
810, 811, 812, 813, 820, 821, 822, 823, 824, 825, 833, 845, 848, 882, 887, 892, 894,
1846, 1850.
LEE-ON-SOLENT – 700H, 700W, 701, 702, 703, 705, 708, 710, 712, 716, 728C,
737X, 739, 746, 752, 753, 754, 760, 763, 764, 764B, 765, 770, 771, 772, 773, 776,
778, 780, 781, 782, 783, 784, 787, 793, 798, 799, 800, 801, 802, 803, 804, 805, 807,
808, 809, 810, 811, 812, 813, 814, 815, 816, 817, 818, 819, 820, 821, 823, 824, 825,
826, 827, 828, 829, 830, 831, 832, 833, 835, 836, 837, 841, 842, 845, 847, 848, 849,
850, 854, 856, 878, 881, 884, 885, 886, 887, 888, 891, 892, 894, 895, 897, 1700, 1701,
1702, 1703, 1791, 1792, 1831.
WORTHY DOWN – 700, 734, 739, 755, 756, 757, 763, 774, 800, 803, 806, 807, 808,
814, 815, 825, 838, 858.

Appendix C

THE SQUADRONS OF THE ROYAL AIR FORCE AND THE UNITS OF THE
UNITED STATES ARMY AIR FORCE THAT WERE BASED AT THE
ADVANCED LANDING GROUNDS

BISTERNE – 371st Fighter Group of the 9th Tactical Air Force.
LYMINGTON – 50th Fighter Group of the 9th Tactical Air Force.
NEEDS ORE POINT – 193, 197, 257, 266.
WINKTON – 404th Fighter Group of the 9th Tactical Air Force.

Appendix D

THE MAIN LUFTWAFFE UNITS USED IN THE ASSAULT
ON THE AIRFIELDS
ORDER OF BATTLE – 13th AUGUST 1940

LUFTFLOTTE 2 – BRUSSELS – Commanded by Generalfeldmarschall Albert Kesselring.
KAMPFGESCHWADER 1–2–3–4–40–53–76.
    Equipment: Heinkel HE111 – Dornier DO17 – Focke Wulfe FW200.
STUKAGESCHWADER 1.
    Equipment: Junkers JU87B 'Stuka'.
LEHRGESCHWADER 1–2.
    Equipment: Junkers JU87B 'Stuka' – Messerschmitt BF109E.
JAGDGESCHWADER 3–26–51–52–54.
    Equipment: Messerschmitt BF109E.
ZERSTÖRERGESCHWADER 26–76.
    Equipment: Messerschmitt BF110.
ERPROBUNGS GRUPPE 210.
    Equipment: Messerschmitt BF109E – Messerschmitt BF110.
KAMPFGRUPPE 100–106.
    Equipment: Heinkel HE111.
KUSTENFLIEGERGRUPPE 106.
    Equipment: Heinkel HE115 – Dornier DO18 – Junkers JU88D – Heinkel HE111.
LUFTFLOTTE 3 – PARIS – Commanded by Generalfeldmarschall Hugo Sperrle.
KAMPFGESCHWADER 1–27–51–54–55.
    Equipment: Heinkel HE111 – Junkers JU88A.
STUKAGESCHWADER 1–2–3–77.
    Equipment: Junkers JU87B 'Stuka' – Dornier DO17 – Heinkel HE111.
LEHRGESCHWADER 1–2.
    Equipment: Junkers JU88A – Messerschmitt BF110 – Dornier DO17F.
JAGDGESCHWADER 2–27–53.
    Equipment: Messerschmitt BF109E.
ZERSTÖRERGESCHWADER 2.
    Equipment: Messerschmitt BF110.
KAMPFGRUPPE 806.
    Equipment: Junkers JU88A – Messerschmitt BF110 – Dornier DO17 – Henschell 126A.
In addition to the two main Luftflottes, Luftflotte 5 operated from Stavanger in Norway for attacks on east coast shipping and the east coast airfields.

Appendix E

GLOSSARY FOR LUFTWAFFE UNITS

Jagdgeschwader	– Fighter Units.
Kampfgeschwader	– Bomber Units.
Zerstorergeschwader	– Long Range Fighter Groups.
Erprobungs Gruppe 210	– Experimental Test Wing 210.
Lehrgeschwader	– Instructional/Operational Development Group.
Stukageschwader	– Dive-Bombing Groups.
Kustenfliegergruppe	– Maritime Luftwaffe Units.
Kampfgruppe	– Coastal Units.

Appendix F

GLOSSARY FOR GERMAN AIRCREW RANKS

Oberst	– (Obst)	Colonel.
Oberstleutnant	– (Obstlt)	Lieutenant Colonel.
Major	– (Maj)	Major.
Hauptmann	– (Hpt)	Captain.
Oberleutnant	– (Oblt)	1st Lieutenant.
Leutnant	– (Lt)	2nd Lieutenant.
Fahnenjunkeroffizier	– (Fhnjr)	Officer Cadet.
Hauptfeldwebel	– (Hptfw)	Sergeant Major.
Oberfeldwebel	– (Ofw)	Flight Sergeant.
Feldwebel	– (Fw)	Sergeant.
Unteroffizier	– (Uffz)	Corporal.
Flieger	– (Flg)	Aircraftsman.

AC	– Army Command
AFC	– Air Force Cross
AI	– Airborne Interception
ALG	– Advanced Landing Ground
ASR	– Air Sea Rescue
AVM	– Air Vice Marshal
BEF	– British Expeditionary Force
CH	– Chain Home (Radar)
CHL	– Chain Home Low (Low Radar)
CIRCUS	– Fighter escorted bombing raid to attract the enemy
CO	– Commanding Officer
DFC	– Distinguished Flying Cross
DH	– De Havilland
DIVER	– Operations against the V1 Rocket
DSO	– Distinguished Service Order
EFTS	– Elementary Flying Training School
ELG	– Emergency Landing Ground
E&RFTS	– Elementary and Reserve Flying Training School
ETPS	– Empire Test Pilots School
FIDO	– Fog Investigation Dispersal Operation
Flt/Lt	– Flight Lieutenant
F/O	– Flying Officer
G/Capt	– Group Captain
GCI	– Ground Controlled Interception
HE	– High Explosive
Lt/Cdr	– Lieutenant Commander
NOBALL	– Rocket and Flying Bomb Sites
P/O	– Pilot Officer
RAMROD	– Day bomber raids escorted by fighters
RANGER	– Deep penetration flights for targets of opportunity
RCAF	– Royal Canadian Air Force
RDF	– Radio Direction Finding
RFC	– Royal Flying Corps
RHUBARB	– Low level strike operation carried out in occupied Europe
ROC	– Royal Observer Corps
RODEO	– Fighter Sweep
Sqd/Ldr	– Squadron Leader
TAF	– Tactical Air Force
USAAF	– United States Army Air Force
USAF	– United States Air Force
Wg/Cdr	– Wing Commander

ACKNOWLEDGEMENTS

I acknowledge with grateful thanks all the individuals and organisations who have assisted me in the writing of this book.

Mrs P A Elliot, Mrs J Baker, Mr James Moore, Mr D H F Price, Mr H Wallace, Mr L A Upton, Mr T Dowland, Captain J R Cross AAC, Mr W G Ramsey, Mr C Samson, Mr L Pilkington, RAF Odiham, RAF Middle Wallop and the Army Air Corps Centre, Imperial War Museum, RAF Museum Hendon, Portsmouth Publishing and Printing Co, Hampshire Record Office, Plaistow Pictorial, Mr John Shorter.

If I have omitted to mention any person or organisation please accept my sincere apologies. Finally thanks go to my wife, as much for her patience as for her proof-reading.

R.J.B.

BIBLIOGRAPHY

During my research I consulted various works. I list them below with grateful thanks to the authors.

RAF Squadrons – W/Cdr C G Jefford (Airlife 1988)
Squadrons of the RAF – James J Halley (Air Britain 1980)
The Blitz – Then and Now, After the Battle Volumes 1 and 3 – Winston G Ramsey (1987)
Squadrons of the Fleet Air Arm – Ray Sturtivant (Air Britain 1984)
Action Stations 9 – C Ashworth (Patrick Stephens 1985)
The Narrow Margin – D Wood and D Dempster (Hutchinson 1961)
Aircraft of the RAF – Owen Thetford (Putnam 1962)
British Naval Aircraft since 1912 – Owen Thetford (Putnam 1962)
Eagle Day – Richard Collier (Hodder & Stoughton 1966)
Hampshire's War – Hampshire Record Office
Night Fighter – C F Rawnsley & Robert Wright (William Collins and Sons 1957)
Dowding and the Battle of Britain – Robert Wright (Macdonald & Co)
Dieppe August 19th – Eric Maguire (Jonathan Cape 1963)

INDEX